KNOW THYSELF
USING THE SYMBOLS OF
FREEMASONRY TO IMPROVE YOUR LIFE

KNOW THYSELF
USING THE SYMBOLS OF FREEMASONRY TO IMPROVE YOUR LIFE

MICHAEL SCHIAVELLO

Lewis Masonic

About the author

Michael Schiavello was born in Melbourne, Australia in 1975. He is a best-selling author, award-winning feature writer and an international television sports broadcaster.

Known as 'The Voice' he has commentated sports events in more than 20 countries, including the 2008 Olympic Games in Beijing. He is the host of 'The Voice Versus' interview show on US television network, AXS TV, where his guests have included Steven Seagal, Sugar Ray Leonard, Hulk Hogan, George Foreman, Stone Cold Steve Austin and Dana White. His feature writing has appeared in more than 50 publications worldwide.

Michael was initiated into Freemasonry in 2009 and raised to Master Mason in 2010, in Deepdene-Balwyn Lodge No. 275, in Melbourne, Australia.

In 2011, Michael relocated to Las Vegas for his television career. There he became a 32nd Degree Mason of the Ancient and Accepted Scottish Rite, and a member of the Royal Arch, Cryptic Council and Knights Templar of the York Rite of Freemasonry.

Michael is the Worshipful Master of Daylite Lodge No. 44 in Las Vegas, Nevada. He also holds a Certificate of Masonic Education from the Victorian Lodge of Research under the United Grand Lodge of Victoria, Australia.

First published 2016
Reprinted 2018, 2021

ISBN 978 0 85318 523 9

All rights reserved. No part of this book may be reproduced or transmitted in any form or by any means, electronic or mechanical, including photocopying, recording, scanning or by any information storage and retrieval system, on the internet or elsewhere, without permission from the Publisher in writing.

© Michael Schiavello 2016

Published by Lewis Masonic

an imprint of Ian Allan Publishing Ltd, Shepperton, Middx TW17 8AS.
Printed in England.

Visit the Lewis Masonic website at www.lewismasonic.co.uk

Copyright
Illegal copying and selling of publications deprives authors, publishers and booksellers of income, without which there would be no investment in new publications. Unauthorised versions of publications are also likely to be inferior in quality and contain incorrect information. You can help by reporting copyright infringements and acts of piracy to the Publisher or the UK Copyright Service.

Picture Credits
Every effort has been made to identify and correctly attribute photographic credits. Should any error have occurred this is entirely unintentional.

Contents

Foreword 7
Introduction 9

Ancient teachers and philosophers 15
Isn't it all secret? 19
How symbolism works 23
The Divine spark – You're a Real G 27
Unleashed! – the Cable Tow 33
Real men wear aprons 40
It's your time – the 24in Gauge 49
Keep chipping away – the Common Gavel 57
What's the point? – the Point within a Circle 64
The bouncer at the door of your mind – the Tyler 73
All a buzz – the Beehive 82
The only way is up – the winding staircase 90
Black and white – the Mosaic Pavement 100
Ssssh – silence and secrecy 108
The Universe's Google – the pencil 118
From darkness – light 126
To see or not see – the All-Seeing Eye 138
No bones about it – the Skull and Crossbones 144
Love rocks – the Ashlars 153
Putting it all into practice – internalising the external 162

Appendix 1 – Famous Masons 164
Appendix 2 – the Three Masonic Degrees 167

Footnotes 168
Index 173

Foreword

I first met Michael Schiavello in San Jose, California in June 2010. He passed by me backstage at the HP Pavilion, where we were both broadcasting an event, and I gestured to the Masonic lapel pin on his left breast.

'Are you a Mason?' I asked.

'I am,' he answered.

'I'm not,' I said, 'but it's something I'm interested in.'

'You should look into it,' Michael said. 'It will change your life.'

Shortly after, I joined Hamilton Lodge #664 in Bettendorf, Iowa, and I am now Worshipful Master of the lodge.

I was inspired to join Freemasonry for a number of reasons, chief among those being the fact that so many great men in history were Masons. These were pivotal individuals in almost every sector of society who particularly opposed tyranny and oppression, and championed self-improvement and the strength of the individual as part of the many.

As I became a Freemason, I recognised many similarities between Masonry and the martial arts. Paying attention to detail is the key to understanding both. Studying techniques and game plans in martial arts is something that takes a great deal of patience and dedication. There are moments when a lightbulb goes off in my head and I say, 'I finally understand this!' I then realise that I was only touching the surface of true understanding. Studying Masonic symbolism has the same effect.

In learning about Masonic symbolism, I have awakening moments, but I know I'm only scratching the surface of understanding the subject. If Freemasonry is a metaphor for life, then I am also only scratching the surface of understanding life. Armed with Masonic instruction, however, I feel I am well equipped for the journey.

On our weekly travels across the United States and Canada in our broadcasting work, Michael and I have been fortunate to visit various Masonic lodges. The men we have met in these lodges hail from all walks of life, from a Mason in Kentucky who sold carnivorous plants for a living to a Mason in New Mexico who oversaw the cross-country transportation of nuclear arms. They were enlightened individuals who, regardless of race, colour, creed or social status, shared a common bond – a mystic tie. These good men sought to become better men through the application of Freemasonry in their lives.

While on the road, Michael and I often find ourselves engaging in deep conversations about Freemasonry and the role it plays in developing our self-awareness and helping us become the best we can be. For the past few years, Michael has shared with me his writings on various Masonic subjects, some of which I have delivered as lectures in my lodge and are found in this book. Each time we talk and every time I read his words, my thought process is challenged and my mind opens up to new and wonderful possibilities for my personal enhancement.

Freemasonry has enabled me to better know who I am. As Michael states in the opening of this book, to know thyself is a call to action for us to make the most of the life we are blessed with, not to live in ignorance of who we are and who we can truly be. Michael's writings on Masonic symbolism, and how you can employ them in your day-to-day life, will help you answer this call to action to better know yourself.

— **Pat Miletich**, UFC Hall of Fame Fighter, Television Broadcaster and Freemason

Introduction
Getting to know me

Self-reverence, self-knowledge, self-control; these three alone lead one to sovereign power.

— Alfred Lord Tennyson

What is the meaning of life? Do you only exist to survive? What is existence? Is life defined by what you eat and drink, whom you sleep with, where you work, how much money you earn, the things you buy and the children you breed?

Is this life?

If these are the parts of life, is the whole of life greater than the sum of its parts? Are you living the best life you can?

Do you ever wonder if there is more to life? Perhaps, just maybe, there's more to you than your bank account, your looks, your friends and family. Perhaps there's something deeper than all of this, something you can't see or touch but exists in you.

Is there an immaterial component to your make up? Something more than flesh, bone, blood, and the hydrogen, carbon, nitrogen and other elements which make up your physical self?

If life is more than your physical being — something greater than what you can see or touch — what is it? What does it mean? And how do you find it?

You might not readily admit it over a beer with friends, but these questions have skipped through your mind at one time or another. There's got to be more to life, right?

The meaning of life has been debated since time immemorial. Thousands of answers and millions of pages in countless books are devoted to its answer. But perhaps the best answer to this timeless question is the adage 'Know Thyself', which may also be the most powerful instruction ever given.

Legend tells us the Seven Sages inscribed these words on the forecourt of the Temple of Apollo at Delphi. Who were these sages? Also known as the Seven Wise Men, they were considered the most enlightened men in ancient Greece. The Seven Sages were:

Bias of Priene — a politician and legislator

Cleobulus of Lindos — governor of Lindos
Solon of Athens — a legislator who framed the laws for Athenian democracy
Chilon of Sparta — a politician who militarised Sparta
Thales of Miletus — the first well-known philosopher and mathematician
Pittacus of Mytilene — governor of Mytilene and Myrsilus
Periander of Corinth — ruler of Corinth, responsible for its golden age of stability

The earliest mention of the Seven Sages appears in Plato's *Protagoras* in which Socrates says: 'There are some, both at present and of old, who recognised that spartanising is much more a love of wisdom than a love of physical exercise, knowing that the ability to utter such [brief and terse] remarks belongs to a perfectly educated man. Among these were Thales of Miletus, and Pittacus of Mytilene, and Bias of Priene, and our own Solon, and Cleobulus of Lindus, and Myson of Chenae, and the seventh of them was said to be Chilon of Sparta. They all emulated and admired and were students of Spartan education, could tell their wisdom was of this sort by the brief but memorable remarks they each uttered when they met and jointly the first fruits of their wisdom to Apollo in his shrine at Delphi, writing what is on every man's lips: *Know thyself*, and *Nothing too much*.'[1]

At the Temple of Apollo, the priestess Pythia answered all questions asked of her, regardless of the seeker's social status. Farmers sought answers on when to plant seeds, as much as leaders sought answers about when to declare war. However, the Temple of Apollo was more than a glorified crystal ball. It was a gathering place for men of various religious inclinations to come together and discuss their beliefs. Scholars congregated at Delphi to discuss their findings, and it became a hub of intellectual inquiry. Political and social rivals met in peace to negotiate desirable outcomes to their differences. It may be said that the Temple of Apollo was the model for the modern Masonic lodge. Freemasonry welcomes men of every race, colour and creed who are strong in character and have sound morals. They gather in its lodges, share thoughts and engage in fellowship to better themselves.

The oracle delivered by Pythia was often shrouded in doublespeak, incomprehensible to commoners and reliant on interpretation. Take, for example, this answer as to whether an individual should engage in battle: 'You will go you will return not in the battle you will perish.'

On face value, the oracle is informing the questioner that he will die if he engages in said battle. However, place a comma in one of two places within Pythia's oracle and a dual meaning is discovered. A comma placed before the word 'not' suggests that the questioner will return from battle: 'You will go you will return, not in the battle you will perish.'

A comma placed after the word 'not' suggests that the questioner will perish in battle: 'You will go you will return not, in the battle you will perish.'

Such is life. Right? One man's trash is another man's treasure, as one man's comma is the difference between anticipating life or death in battle. Life is based on interpretation. Take, for instance, this mathematics problem:

2+2 = 4
However, 3+1 also equals 4.
So too does 5-1 and 2x2.
So which method of arriving at '4' is correct?

All interpretations are correct no matter the method of determination. The destination is the same.

Thales of Miletus (624-546 BCE) provided the inscription 'Know Thyself' above the temple at Delphi. A pre-Socratic Greek philosopher from Miletus in Asia Minor, Thales is known as the grandfather of Western philosophy who attempted to explain the world and all in it without reference to mythology. He provided practical explanations for cosmological events that had previously been explained by way of supernatural entities. His questioning approach to the understanding of heavenly phenomena was the beginning of Greek astronomy. Thales' hypotheses were new and bold, and in freeing phenomena from godly intervention, he paved the way towards scientific endeavour. Founder of the Milesian school of natural philosophy, he gave birth to the scientific method, and created the first Western enlightenment. He is likewise regarded as the first mathematician, and the 'Father of Science.'

From Ancient Egypt to modern-day philosophy classes, Thales' adage 'Know Thyself' has become the centrepiece for study and reflection. Said Thales: 'The most difficult thing in life is to know yourself.'

Of self-knowledge, the Ancient Egyptians said, 'Man, know thyself, and thou shalt know the gods. The body is the temple of the god within you; therefore it is said, Man, know thyself.'

Aristotle claimed, 'Knowing yourself is the beginning of all wisdom.'

Later Socrates stated, 'Wisdom begins with wonder; the wonder that emanates from developing knowledge of oneself before knowledge of anything else.'

Lao Tzu, a philosopher and poet of Ancient China, who was born about 100 years before Socrates, said, 'Knowing others is intelligence; knowing yourself is true wisdom. Mastering others is strength; mastering yourself is true power.'

In the Bhagavad Gita it states, 'This is true knowledge, to seek the Self as the true end of wisdom always. To seek anything else is ignorance.'

Why is self-knowledge paramount to your existence? As English author Aldous Huxley wrote, 'There is only one corner of the universe you can be certain of improving, and that's your own self.'

Knowing thyself takes effort. It is a lifelong pursuit. Huxley noted that most of us remain ignorant of ourselves. To know thyself is a call to action. It is a command for you to make the most of life, and not to ignore who you are and who you can truly be.

To know thyself is to know what makes you tick and what makes you think. Ultimately, knowing thyself is to reveal the spark at your centre, wherein your true self exists. Call this centre what you like — your soul, inner self, divine spark, inner spirit, quintessence, source, élan vital — it doesn't matter. Just know that a spark is there, as the greatest teachers have taught throughout history.

To reach this centre you must chip away at your outer shell, at your ego, lusts, passions and desires — your animal self — and bring to light that which is kept hidden in darkness. It's like tunnelling through a mountain with an icepick, bit by bit, chipping away until you reach a cave at the centre of the mountain wherein lies an amazing treasure. Revelation of your inner light — your centre — is illumination. As C. S. Lewis wrote: 'You don't have a soul. You are a soul. You have a body.'

To know thyself is a mission statement to make your good self better. This is the core teaching of Freemasonry. *Ex Tenebris Lux* — From Darkness, Light.

To know thyself requires finding a path to greater knowledge. Following any path in life requires direction. We are all tourists walking a giant map, flipping it this way and the other, figuring out where we are heading. We constantly ask ourselves, 'Where am I?' and our map gives us an arrow, a star and giant letters that read, 'YOU ARE HERE.' We then decide where we want to go to next, relying on the map to get us there. Without a map, we may get lost. Some of us with a better sense of natural direction may get to our destination even without a map, but we will not get there as effectively as when using a map.

As the famed physicist, Isaac Newton, observed in his first law of motion, 'An object at rest stays at rest and an object in motion stays in motion with the same speed and in the same direction unless acted upon by an unbalanced force.'

Don't let unbalanced forces upset your course. Stay in motion and elevate your life above mediocrity. Choose advancement over rest, in all aspects of life. You don't exist merely to survive, but to progress, transcend and conquer. Your challenge today is to conquer yesterday's self.

Every system of teaching offers a map with directions for advancement. Advancement leads to illumination, which is a necessary part of life. One doesn't join a Karate dojo to stay a white belt forever, just as one shouldn't be an idle spectator in life. Never mind your social status, your genetics, the size of your bank account or the size of your biceps. There exists within you something more than a purely material being. The means to attain this knowledge, the knowledge of thyself, is deep inside — you just have to reach it. As Hindu monk and philosopher Swami Vivekananda said, 'All knowledge is within us. All perfection is there already'.

Carl Jung, the renowned Swiss founder of analytical psychology, said, 'Who looks outside dreams. Who looks inside awakens'. It is time to look inside yourself for answers to life's questions. It is time to get to know thyself.

For centuries, Freemasonry has provided a map for men to follow on their path to self-improvement. It is a system of teaching rooted in the mystery schools of Ancient Egypt, infused with the ideas of the great Greek philosophers, impressed with lessons communicated by teachers before the Common Era (BCE), through to the Renaissance, and is still relevant today.

Freemasonry is not a religion nor a substitute for religion. It requires that its members believe in a Supreme Being — atheists cannot become Freemasons, and you'll understand why after reading this book — but does not advocate a sectarian faith or practice. It has no dogma or theological doctrine, and forbidding religious discussion during its meetings does not allow a Masonic theological doctrine to develop. Freemasonry offers no sacraments and does not claim to lead to salvation.

Freemasonry is not a cult. It is not a secret society, a new world order, a boys' club, nor a watering hole for Don Quixote-like octogenarians. Freemasonry is a 'beautiful system of morality, veiled in allegory and illustrated by symbols' and much more.

At its heart, Freemasonry is a deeply personal pursuit and means something different to each of its members. It is a commitment by an individual to pursue a time-honoured system of instruction for improving himself in mind, body, and soul. It is a science, philosophy, art and universal knowledge that provides an understanding of how we fit into the universe and how the universe fits into us. Freemasonry is often referred to as 'The Craft'. 'Craft' is defined as *to make or manufacture with skill and careful attention to detail.* Freemasons manufacture their selves with skill and attention to detail, and thus every Freemason is truly a Craftsman.

Through Masonic knowledge of self-improvement, a person comes to know themselves and their function in existence, and improve upon that existence for a better station in life. Its lessons are ageless and are the same lessons communicated by the greatest teachers such as Plato, Pythagoras, Aristotle, Socrates, Jesus, Confucius, Lao Tzu, Gandhi and Roger Bacon.

Masonic author Walter Wilmshurst writes that the new Mason 'who aspires to mastership will become conscious of an increase of perceptive faculty and understanding: he will become aware of having tapped a previously unsuspected source of power, giving him enhanced mental strength and self-confidence; there will become observable in him developing graces of character, speech and conduct that were previously foreign to him'.[2]

At the core of Masonic teaching is the use of symbols to impress on the mind deep and powerful lessons about self-improvement and the mystery of the inner self. This book will expose you to several key symbols of Masonic teaching. At first, some may seem trivial, even a little hokey. After all, how does a pencil, a beehive or a rock convey any profound teaching about personal illumination? Trust me, they do.

You are about to embark on a wondrous journey through Masonic symbolism and how you can apply these symbols to your everyday life. It is a journey undertaken by millions before you. Many of them acquired this knowledge without joining the ranks of Freemasonry and got hold of a map some other way. Others, including actors, politicians, kings, billionaires, astronauts, presidents and pop stars all joined the ranks of Freemasonry to get a hold of their own road map. Be it through Freemasonry or some other path of learning, they all shared the same destination. It is your destination too. It begins now and ends with knowing exactly who you are. For as Lao Tzu said more than 2500 years ago, 'He who knows others is wise. He who knows himself is enlightened.'

Ancient teachers and philosophers

A teacher affects eternity. He can never tell where his influence stops.
— Henry Adams

In the following pages, you will receive lessons, tidbits and insights from a number of ancient teachers and philosophers. Their lessons live on hundreds and even thousands of years after their deaths. Here are a few of the teachers and philosophers you will come across in this book.

ARISTOTLE
384-322 BCE
A student of Plato and a teacher of Alexander the Great. Founded his own school, the Lyceum, in Athens in 335 BCE. Laid much of the groundwork for Western philosophy. The first person in Western history to argue that there is a hierarchy to all life in the Universe.

He said: We are what we repeatedly do. Excellence, then, is not an act, but a habit.

GAUTAMA SIDDHARTHA BUDDHA
c 563 BCE
Spiritual leader and teacher whose teachings form the foundation of Buddhism. Became the 'Buddha' (enlightened one / he who is awake) after long meditation under a Bodhi tree in which answers to his questions on life and the universe were revealed.

He said: No one saves us but ourselves. No one can and no one may. We ourselves must walk the path.

CONFUCIUS
551-479 BCE
Influential teacher, philosopher and political identity. His teachings focused on setting educational standards, and creating rules of ethics, particularly espousing the Golden Rule of loving others while exercising self-discipline.

He said: To practice five things under all circumstances constitutes perfect virtue; these five are gravity, generosity of soul, sincerity, earnestness, and kindness.

LAO TZU
Lived between 6th century and 4th century BCE
At a time when Greece and Southern Italy had Pythagoras, and India had Buddha, China had the influential teacher, Lao Tzu. He wrote the *Tao Te Ching* and founded Taoism. Promoted a non-aggressive and harmonious way of life, acting in accordance with nature and the laws that govern the natural and universal order.

He said: Without darkness, there can be no light.

PLATO
428-348 BCE
Founder of The Academy in Athens, one of the first schools of higher learning in the Western world. His teachings focused on mathematics, beauty, equality, justice, political philosophy, theology, aesthetics, epistemology, cosmology and language. Created the foundation for modern democracy.

He said: We can easily forgive a child who is afraid of the dark; the real tragedy of life is when men are afraid of the light.

PYTHAGORAS
582-500 BCE
Mathematician, teacher and philosopher. Best known for the Pythagorean Theorem relating to right angle triangles. Also determined the movement of the planets and stars, and the relationship of music to mathematics. Founder of the Pythagorean Brotherhood, which taught secrecy, vegetarianism, periods of food abstinence and silence, refusal to eat beans, refusal to wear animal skins, celibacy, self-examination, immortality, and reincarnation.

He said: Choose rather to be strong of soul than strong of body.

JESUS OF NAZARETH
7-2 BCE-33CE
Central figure in Christianity whose teachings are recorded in the New Testament of the Holy Bible. These teachings include: God's love for Mankind; the Kingdom of God; compassion and forgiveness; loving your neighbour as yourself. Based on the

number of students worldwide throughout the centuries, Jesus may be regarded as the most successful teacher in history.

He said: You have heard that it was said, 'eye for eye, and tooth for tooth.' But I tell you, do not resist an evil person. If someone strikes you on the right cheek, turn to him the other also.

HILEL
110 BCE-10 CE
Jewish religious leader associated with the development of the Mishnah and the Talmud. Founder of the House of Hilel school for Tannaim. One of the most important figures in Jewish history.

He said: That which is hateful to you, do not do to your fellow. That is the whole Torah; the rest is the explanation; go and learn.

ALCMAEON
Born around 5th century BCE
Greek medical writer, philosopher and scientist. Had tremendous impact on his successors, including Plato who adopted Alcmaeon's argument for the immortality of the soul and accepted his view that the brain is the seat of intelligence.

He said: Men perish because they cannot join the beginning with the end.

EPICTETUS
55-135CE
Greek philosopher whose teachings carried religious tones. Believed all men, as rational beings, are sons of God and are kindred in nature with the divinity. Taught that all external events are determined by fate and are beyond one's control, however one is responsible for his actions, which can be controlled through self-discipline.

He said: It's not what happens to you, but how you react to it that matters.

MAHAVIRA
599-527 BCE
Central figure of the religion of Jainism. Renounced his princely status and life of riches, and spent more than twelve years in silence and meditation to conquer his desires and attachments. Taught non-violence, non-stealing, chastity, truthfulness,

and detachment from people, places and material objects.

He said: Live and allow others to love; hurt no one; life is dear to all living beings.

XUN ZI
310-237 BCE
One of the three great Confucian philosophers of China's classical period. Wrote the *Xunzi*, a book comprising 32 chapters

He said: The person attempting to travel two roads at once will get nowhere.

SYMEON THE NEW THEOLOGIAN
949-1022 CE
A poet who embodied the mystical tradition. One of three saints given the title 'Theologian' by the Orthodox Church. Taught that one could experience God through 'theoria' — the personal contemplation of God.

He said: Strive for peace with all men, and for the holiness without which no one will see the Lord (Heb. 12:14), Why did he say 'strive'? Because it is not possible for us to become holy and to be saints in an hour! We must therefore progress from modest beginnings toward holiness and purity. Even were we to spend a thousand years in this life we should never perfectly attain it. Rather we must always struggle for it every day, as if mere beginners.

Isn't it all secret?

The human heart has hidden treasures. In secret kept, in silence sealed; The thoughts, the hopes, the dreams, the pleasures, whose charms were broken if revealed.
— Charlotte Bronte

How many times have you heard Freemasonry referred to as a secret society? Many, I'm sure. The fact of the matter is that much of Freemasonry is not secret at all, and that which is secret is so for very good reason.

If Freemasons are part of a secret society, how do you explain the enormous square and compasses that adorn their buildings, clearly indicating to passers-by that such buildings are Masonic meeting places? Would a true secret society use such a public display of its location?

If Freemasons are such secretive characters, dwelling in the shadows of society and infiltrating the upper echelons of the corporate world without anyone being the wiser to their presence, how do you explain why so many Masons proudly wear rings, lapel pins and caps with Masonic logos for all to see? Why do so many Masons drive cars with Masonic licence plates or bumper stickers? Would a secret society take part in public parades in full regalia?

Would a secret society lend its names to such establishments as a Shriner's Health Clinic or a Freemason's Hospital?

If Freemasonry was truly secret, would you be able to buy Masonic mugs, pocket knives, scarves, neckties, saucers and letter openers?

Would a personality such as NBA star Shaquille O'Neal go on television and blatantly show off his Masonic ring if Freemasonry was truly a secret society?

Would other well-known personalities such as Michael Richards, John Wayne, Clark Gable, Nat 'King' Cole, Oliver Hardy, Louis Armstrong, Don Rickles, and Leonard Cohen all make public a group to which they were members if that group was truly secret?

Simply put, if the aim of Freemasonry centres on remaining a secret to the outside world, it is a major failure.

Freemasonry is not a secret society; it is a society with secrets. There *are* secrets in Freemasonry, but despite what the conspiracy theorists would have you believe, these secrets do not entail the location of the Holy Grail, the design of the Egyptian pyramids or the propagation of a New World Order. Freemasons don't know who killed JFK, are not aware of the entrance to Hollow Earth, and do not take orders from alien overlords.

So what are the secrets of Freemasonry? They are, at their most basic, the 'signs of recognition', both physical and verbal, which Masons across the world use to prove and recognise one another. Known as 'grips' or 'tokens', a Masonic handshake enables one Mason to know another 'in the light' and 'in the dark'. It's pretty simple, really. By shaking each other's hand in a variety of ways, a Freemason identifies another Freemason — a man he has a common connection to – and the level of Masonic education that Freemason has attained (There are different 'signs' and 'words' of recognition for all levels in Freemasonry).

'But secret handshakes and methods of greeting each other are sinister', cry the conspiracy theorists.

By this reasoning, billions of people around the world who use particular methods of greeting one another as a means of identifying a connection of commonality are sinister in their nature, including the Boy Scouts, college fraternities and sororities, and kids playing in tree houses. ('You can't come in and play unless you know the secret knock and password!')

Okay, but why do the handshakes and passwords need to be secret? Why can't they be told to non-Masons? I'll answer that question with another question: why should they be?

A Masonic handshake or password is like a PIN code. Your PIN is a secret numeric combination known only to you and your bank's computer system, and is a means the bank uses to recognise you as the owner of the account you're accessing. Once your PIN becomes public, anyone can access your funds.

If you work in a corporate building, you probably have a swipe card or fob to gain access to various offices and file rooms. The swipe card only allows access to those areas that you have permission to enter. If you're denied permission, it's because you're not privy to the information behind the door.

Anti-Masonic lobbyists argue that signs of recognition are proof that Masons are hiding something they don't want the world to know. In fact, quite the opposite is true. Every Mason I know openly encourages people to join their local lodge and experience the camaraderie and learning Freemasonry promotes. There's an old saying about joining Freemasonry: 'To be one, ask one'. Most Freemasons will gladly talk your ear off about the time-honoured institution to which they belong and openly encourage you to join its ranks.

Some Freemasons, whom I like to call 'Postcard Masons' (more about them later), like to play the 'secret society' card. They smugly tell friends and family they can't divulge anything about Freemasonry. If a Freemason ever tells you this, it's likely you're dealing with a massive ego and such a person is best avoided. The only secrets a Freemason is *not* permitted to tell a non-Mason (known as a 'cowan' in Mason-speak) are the modes of recognition – that is all! In adhering to the solemn obligations taken by this author, none of these modes of recognition are divulged in this book.

Masonic modes of recognition – the handshakes, the passwords, the signs – can be found on the internet, but don't get too excited thinking that a simple Google search will enable you to crack the shell of this timeless organisation. To know the signs of recognition – the physical secrets – is not to know Freemasonry; just as reading an article on how to do an emergency repair of a leaking abdominal aortic aneurysm does not qualify you as a brain surgeon.

It is one thing to read words on paper and look at pictures; it is another thing altogether to experience something for yourself. Just as you can't truly know about love and relationships by reading about them, so too can you not truly know about Freemasonry by reading about the subject. That said, advice columns, books, lectures and the like all have their place. They challenge your thinking, expand your mind and make you question your life, your surroundings, your actions and the consequences of those actions. This book does the same. While you cannot truly comprehend the astoundingly deep teachings of Masonry unless you feel them, the study of Masonic symbols will lead you to a challenging and (hopefully) highly rewarding place. It's time to push the boundaries of your thinking process. Get ready!

Masons do keep secrets, which is not a bad thing. The word 'secret' gets a bad rap, but a secret can be a positive and rewarding thing to possess. Masonic passwords, handshakes and signs of recognition, are kept secret to test the mettle of their possessor's character. There is much to measure in a person by how well he keeps a secret. If a friend confides intimate details of their life, that confidence comes with the expectation that in the spirit of true friendship you won't shout their information from the rooftops or gossip it among others. We entrust secrets to those close to us because we value the relationship and know that come hell or high water, our true friends will not divulge our secrets.

For the individual Mason, the true secret of Freemasonry is so great that it can't possibly be revealed to anyone else. The secret is the personal experience of Freemasonry.

Freemasonry knocks down walls within the psyche. Masonic teaching inserts a key into the subconscious, turns a lock and opens a door; where that door leads is different for each person – it is a personal realisation. Grab a thesaurus and look up synonyms for 'personal' and you will see these words: 'intimate', 'particular', 'special', 'exclusive', 'privy' and 'secret'.

In the following pages, you will learn about Masonic symbolism. Such knowledge is not secret. Symbolism is a method that has long existed for conveying information that cannot be effectively transmitted through words. You will learn how to use this symbolism to improve aspects of your daily life such as time management, positive thinking, appreciation of others, strengthening will power, working together, recognising dualities, and increasing your intellect.

This information has been around for centuries, some of it dating back more than two thousand years and employed by great minds such as Pythagoras, Lao Tzu, Plato and Aristotle. In more recent times, figures like George Washington, Buzz Aldrin, Sugar Ray Robinson, Theodore Roosevelt, Yitzhak Rabin, Winston Churchill, Jesse Jackson, and Billy Graham, were all influenced by Masonic symbols. Walt Disney, Captain James Cook, Lewis and Clark, Mark Twain, Oscar Wilde, Wolfgang Mozart, and Pat 'Mr Miyagi' Morita all took part in Masonic learning. Louis Armstrong, Clark Gable, Peter Sellers, Ernest Borgnine, Billy Wilder, Arnold Palmer, Michael Richards, Richard Prior, Jack Dempsey, and UFC champion Pat Miletich, all benefitted from Masonic instruction.

These men took common symbols such as a pencil, a square, a circle, a beehive, a skull and crossbones, and a sword, and probed deep into the moral lessons they convey. Are these lessons secret? Yes, but only because they are hidden from common view. When you see a pencil, for example, you see an instrument for writing. Any other symbolic lesson conveyed by the pencil is hidden from you until you find it. A secret is only a secret until divulged.

Freemasonry has withstood the test of time. In its current form it dates from the formation of the first Grand Lodge of England in a London tavern in 1717, and before that to the stonemason guilds of the Middle Ages. Trace the origin of Masonic symbolism even further back and it reaches all the way to the Roman schools of mysteries, the teachings of the Cathars, the Kabbalists, the Essenes, the Osirian mysteries of Ancient Egypt, the Sumerians, Phoenicians, and the Socratic mysteries of Ancient Greece. Masonic symbolism brings the essential teachings of the ancient world to a modern audience, of which you are a part.

How symbolism works

We are symbols, and inhabit symbols.

— Ralph Waldo Emerson

Freemasonry is the science of symbolism. However, symbolism is not unique to Freemasonry. Every day, often without realising it, we use symbols to decipher information.

No matter where you are, you will inevitably see a symbol of some kind, designed to transmit information to your brain and ingrain it on your mind in a very direct way. Even on this page, you have already seen the use of two different symbols. Do you know what they are? Here's a clue: you have now seen four.

If you said full stops, commas, a colon, and a question mark, you are correct. A full stop is a symbol that a sentence has ended instead of writing the word 'STOP' as was once used on telegraph services. A comma is a symbol of pause in writing, communicated through a symbol instead of writing the word 'pause' or 'beat'.

Symbols are all around us and instantly convey an abstract idea that would require sentences or even paragraphs of text to relate. We avoid parking our car in a disabled spot by seeing the symbol of a wheelchair painted on the road. We locate restrooms in any public setting by the symbol of a white figure on a blue background. A green light is a symbol to 'go', a red light a symbol to stop and an amber light a symbol to wait or slow down. A picture of a seatbelt flashing overhead on an airplane tells you to fasten your seatbelt. An arrow is a symbol that tells you which direction to take. A dot radiating three arches of increasing size at the top of your computer screen symbolises the strength of your internet connection.

Corporations also use symbols as a means for customers to identify their products. We are all familiar with the McDonalds golden arches, BMW's white propeller spinning in a blue sky, Nike's swoosh, the triple stripe of adidas and the Macy's star. Through symbols, businesses are able to communicate their brand without words, instead ingraining these images on our minds. For example, did you know the adidas triple stripe is actually a mountain range? It symbolises the challenges of life we must all overcome, for which a pair of reliable adidas shoes is helpful.[3] Book lovers will be well aware of the symbol used by online retailer Amazon, which features a curved line under the company name. The line begins under the letter 'A' and finishes under the letter 'Z'. In essence, the symbol is a smile because that is what happens when you realise you can buy everything on Amazon, from A to Z!

A symbol is an object that represents, stands for or suggests an idea, visual image, belief, action, or material entity. Various faiths use symbols to represent their doctrines. When we see a cross, the words 'church' or 'Christian Church' are not necessary – the symbol conveys the message. A synagogue does not need the words 'Jewish Temple' or 'Jewish Synagogue' posted above its entrance – the Star of David serves this purpose symbolically without the use of words.

Freemasonry utilises symbols to convey material, moral, and spiritual lessons on how a person should live their life. Understanding Freemasonry begins with comprehension of its symbols, which make up the heart of Masonic instruction. It is impossible to understand the enormous scope of Masonic thought and teaching without interpretation of its symbols. Common Masonic symbols such as the square and compasses, the plumb line, the common gavel, the 24-inch gauge, the trowel, the beehive, the Ionic, Doric and Corinthian pillars, and the sprig of acacia convey specific messages to the conscious and subconscious mind without the need for words.

Take, for example, the symbol of a trowel. To the non-Mason, a trowel is a tool used by bricklayers to spread cement. To a Mason, a trowel represents the spreading of brotherly love that binds together humanity. A trowel reminds the Mason of his duty as a member of the human race to spread love and affection among all. Copious amounts of text can be written about the importance of spreading love and affection but this simple symbol sums up the moral teaching effectively in one picture.

You may ask, *What about all these evil symbols of the so-called 'illuminati' and Satanists I often read about on the internet?*

Let me make one thing perfectly clear. A symbol is only empowered by your interpretation of it, just as a car is only powered by gas. Without gas, a car is just a shell. Without interpretation, a symbol is just a drawing. A symbol carries as much or as little power as you choose to invest it with.

A triangle drawn with crayons by a four-year-old in kindergarten does not radiate any great power or convey any sublime message or truth. It is, simply, a triangle. To the high school geometry student, the same triangle is symbolic of the Pythagoras Theorem, $a^2 + b^2 = c^2$. To the Freemason, a triangle is symbolic of the complete man in whom the three sides of the triangle represent the three aspects of a person: physical, mental, spiritual; or mind, body and soul. To the Satanist, the triangle – known as a thaumaturgic triangle – is a symbol used for casting spells or summoning demons. A symbol is only as powerful as you allow. Sometimes, in fact most of the time, a triangle is just…a triangle!

Conspiracy theorists are quick to attach sinister significance to most symbols. For example, a pop star dancing on a black and white checkered floor in a video clip is a symbol that the celebrity is in league with satanic forces. By the same reasoning, my ninety-year-old neighbour, a loving grandmother of twelve who attends church every Sunday, must also be in cahoots with the devil. After all, the tiles on her bathroom floor are black and white!

According to the conspiracy theorists, all the basic shapes we learn to draw as children – triangles, squares, circles, stars – are symbols of Satanism or the 'illuminati'. Other innocent symbols such as the sun, the moon, water, arches, pyramids, and even dots are also considered sinister. Why? Because conspiracy theorists empower these symbols as such.

Take, for example, the symbol of retail giant, the Target Corporation. It's a circle with a dot in the middle otherwise known as – a target! But according to conspiracy theorists the logo represents a penis (the dot) inside a vagina (the circle) and is therefore symbolic of pagan phallic worship. To the rest of us the Target logo is simply a target.

Symbols mean to us that which we interpret them to mean. A black cat means bad luck in the USA but good luck in Japan. A cross means little more to a Buddhist than two intersecting lines, but is the central symbol in the Christian belief system.

Symbolic meaning is also attached to numbers. The number seven is considered lucky by most and the number 13 symbolises bad luck. There is even a name for the fear of the number 13: triskaidekaphobia. Those who interpret '13' as a symbol of bad luck will not stay on the 13th floor of a hotel and fear any Friday that falls on the 13th day of the month. Why are they scared? Not because of any proven fact that '13' brings bad luck but because they choose to empower the number 13 as a symbol of misfortune.

Much is written about the secrecy of Freemasonry and its symbols. There is nothing secret about a trowel, compasses, square, pencil, beehive, cube or any other Masonic symbol. We see many of these objects in our daily lives, and for most they remain only objects with no meaning or power. However, once we attach symbolism to these objects, they take on a deeper meaning. Take the beehive as an example. Most see a beehive as the dwelling place of bees. To the Mason, however, a beehive symbolises industry and working together in a structured and well-organised society, as bees do.

Masonic symbols are much like a PowerPoint presentation. Each symbol imports meaning to an embodiment of picture images and data within a specific school of thought[4]. You've heard the saying, 'A picture is worth a thousand words'. This is not a new concept. The symbols of Freemasonry are hundreds of years old at least, and some even older appear in the mystery schools of Ancient Greece and Egypt, employed by the Sumerians, Phoenicians, Persians and Mesopotamians. The point within a circle is a perfect example. This important Masonic symbol closely resembles an Egyptian hieroglyph dated more than 1500 years before the Common Era. Likewise, the square, a key symbol in Freemasonry, dates as far back as the writings of Confucius in 481 BCE.

To understand symbolism and use symbols to improve your life is to share a common link with the sages of old who conveyed their most important lessons through this method. Why did the sages use symbols instead of words?

Carl Jung taught there are concepts beyond the human range of comprehension, which is why religions particularly employ symbolic images. No matter how much we know and how much we can see, touch, hear and taste, our comprehension of things reaches a point from which our conscious knowledge cannot go further. [5]

In the following pages, you will learn the deeper meaning of several Masonic symbols and how to use them to improve your daily life. The key to using Masonic symbols for your personal advancement lies not in reading about the symbols but in *feeling* them. Once you begin to feel the symbol, its effect will be to awaken previously dormant areas of your brain. This awakening serves to heighten thought patterns and increase vibrations of the mind. When you consider that we are all energy, and that energy is all vibration, you begin to realise just how startling an effect the knowledge of symbolism can have on your entire being, and the balancing of your mind, body and soul.

Masons quietly reflect on symbols and ponder their deeper meaning. I encourage you to do the same. Let the symbols in this book sink into your deepest self, so that the lessons attached to them become as ingrained as the McDonald's golden arches when you're in need of a hamburger or the symbol of a wheelchair when looking for a disabled parking spot.

The divine spark
You're a real 'G'

The Divine Light is always in man, presenting itself to the senses and to the comprehension, but man rejects it.

— Giordano Bruno

'Divine spark' is a term you will come across several times in this book. What exactly is your divine spark and why is it so important?

The divine spark is not about believing in a particular religion or following a certain belief. Erase all religious connotations from your mind. Think of your divine spark in terms of something anatomical, which is operative as much as it is speculative or philosophical.

It is hard to believe that a being as amazing as a human is a mere aggregation of matter and elements that work perfectly in an established order. Our body is too complicated to be solely matter. There needs to be something that connects us with something superior and extraordinary, and that something is the divine spark, the sign that we are more than monkey relatives; more than blood, bone and elements in the periodic table. We are invisible energy manifest in flesh.

The divine spark is an energetic charge we receive at the moment of conception, through the miracle of life creation. According to Gnostic beliefs, this spark is a gift from God, which we must activate during our lifetime through actions and experiences. Thus, since it is a divine fragment, it will guide us towards love, harmony, and peace. After our body dies, the spark returns to its creator, that is God, the universe, the super consciousness.

In the centre of the famous Masonic square and compasses is placed the letter 'G'[6]. Masonic ritual tells us the letter G stands for 'God', 'Geometry' and the 'Great Geometrician of the Universe.' The square and compasses are symbolic of you. The compasses represents your spiritual/higher-self sitting above the square, which is symbolic of your material self. The placement of the G at the centre of this symbol represents the divine spark at your centre.

It is no coincidence that G is the seventh letter of the English alphabet; the number seven has long been considered a sacred number by Freemasons, certain religions and ancient mystery schools.

- The energy of the body rises through seven chakras, the seventh being the highest
- God created the world in six days and rested on the seventh day
- Solomon's Temple was completed after seven years
- There are seven days in a week
- Seven tones in a musical scale
- Seven planets of the ancients moving in perfect harmony through the vast expanse of the universe
- The Seven Sages of Ancient Greece
- The Seven Wonders of the World
- The Seven Liberal Arts and Sciences
- The seven stages of alchemical process
- It takes seven Freemasons to make a lodge perfect
- Seven colours in a rainbow

G is the seventh letter of the English alphabet, and the third (3) letter of both the Greek alphabet (Gamma) and Hebrew alphabet (Gimmel). This is important to note as much Masonic symbolism and teaching derives from the ancient mystery schools, of which Greek and Hebrew were the alphabets in employment. The fact that G, therefore, represents two sacred numbers – seven and three – makes it an extraordinary letter. Adding seven and three gives us ten, which to the students of the Pythagorean mystery school was considered the most sacred of all numbers.

The tenth letter of the Hebrew alphabet is Yod, and it is from Yod that all other letters of the alphabet are constructed. Symbolically, Yod represents God, as from God – Supreme Being / Higher Power / The Source – all things are created. With this information in hand, it should come as no surprise that the letter Yod when written resembles the number seven and, sometimes looks like the flame (divine *spark*) of a candle. The number seven, when written like [ℸ] resembles the square of Freemasonry, symbolic of joining of one's spiritual (vertical) and material (horizontal). The same symbol, in reverse, is the Gamma of the Greek alphabet. [Γ]

Freemasonry places the letter G in the centre of the square and compasses, which is exactly where it needs to be as it represents the divine spark at your centre!

Sometimes the letter G is placed within an equilateral triangle (symbol of perfection), others times within a blazing star with five points (a star shaped like a man, the five points representing the head, arms and legs; also the five elements: air, water, fire, earth, ether). When you understand that the G represents your divine spark – the perfect god-part at your centre, an inextinguishable flame – its depiction in an equilateral triangle or blazing star makes complete sense.

The G at your centre

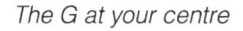

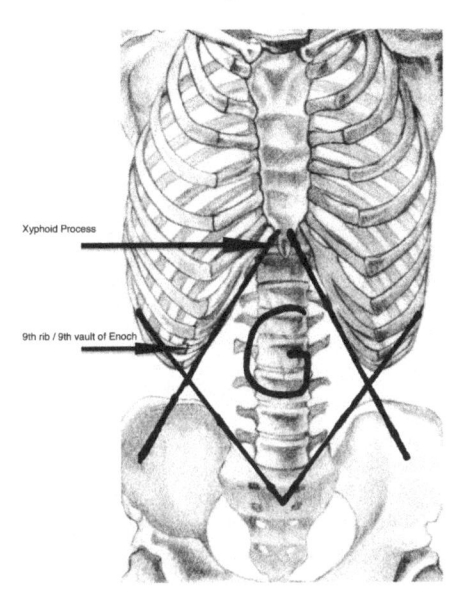

The G also symbolises Geometry, which Freemasons are taught is synonymous with Freemasonry. This is true if one starts with the science of Geometry and then delves deeper. Freemasonry teaches through Geometry that the student may curiously trace Nature through her various windings to her *most concealed recesses*.

There it is!

Through Geometry – or Freemasonry, one being the same as the other – we are able to reveal the innermost parts of nature. This happens through a winding movement, as explained in a later chapter on the winding staircase. Indeed, the letter G winds by design. Through Freemasonry (Geometry) we're able to arrive at the very centre of our nature – our divine spark! Hence the letter G in the centre of the square and compasses tells the Freemason: *You can get here, to your centre, and this is what you'll find!*

Hold on, you may be thinking. *This whole 'centre' thing sounds a little ambiguous. Where exactly is this centre? If Geometry is a precise science, shouldn't there be a precise location for the centre of my being where this divine spark is located?*

The answer to these questions is revealed in the Holy Royal Arch of the York Rite of Freemasonry and the Royal Arch of Solomon (King of the Ninth Arch) of Scottish Rite Freemasonry.

Allegorically, these degrees centre around the building of the second Temple in Jerusalem following the destruction of King Solomon's Temple. While excavating the ground, workmen discover an underground vault built by the prophet Enoch and constructed of nine arches, one on top of the other. Inside the ninth and innermost vault, Enoch placed a cubical block of marble in which he set a triangular plate of gold, encrusted with precious stones and engraved with the ineffable name of God.

It is important to stress here that the story of Enoch's vaults is, as with all Masonic teaching, an allegory. The story appears in the Book of Enoch and in Masonic ritual, but it is not meant to be taken literally. Enoch's vaults lead the workmen to uncover a great hidden treasure: the true name of God. However, this is not a literal name like John, Steven, Jim or Frank. The name of God is the *essence* of God, and that essence of God is the divine spark. One must travel through the nine arches to reach this hidden treasure.

What are the nine arches?

Look at the picture of Enoch's vaults; looks a lot like a rib cage, right?

It does! Only problem is that we have twelve sets of ribs, not nine. Busted!

Enoch's vaults are nine in number because it is at the base of the ninth set of ribs that the treasure is located. At this point in the body lies the transplyoric plane, a horizontal line just above the ninth set of ribs. What lies at the centre of this plane? The solar plexus. Writes influential New Thought[7] lecturer, Julia Seton:

The nine vaults of Enoch. Note how they resemble a rib cage and spine.

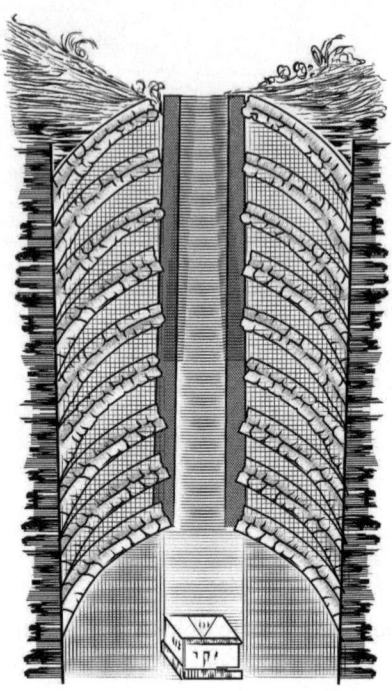

'The Solar Plexus is the home of the ego or the spirit of men; it is the connecting link between man and the Infinite and is the meeting place of the divinely physical, and the physically divine man. From the solar plexus we receive our visions called faith, and when we register them in the field of consciousness of our physical brain, and work them out through scientific human reasoning into tangible expression, they then become facts.'[8]

American New Thought author, Theron Q. Dumont, tells us that we have mistaken our heart as the seat of our emotions, whereas really our emotions stem from the solar plexus.

'One of the great facts concerning the Solar Plexus, or Abdominal Brain … which has been known for centuries by occultists … is this important fact, i.e. that the Solar Plexus is the seat of the emotional nature of Man. In short, that the part popularly held to be played by "the heart", is in reality performed by the Solar Plexus…'[9]

The duodenum resembles the letter G

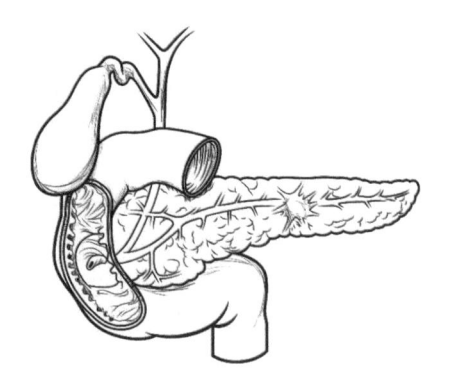

Amazingly, either by sheer coincidence or the genius of a higher intelligence, located at the centre of the solar plexus region is the duodenum. Can you guess what shape the duodenum takes? That of the letter G! If you look at a skeleton of the human body, and view the top of the pelvic bone as a square, and the bottom-most ribs up to the xyphoid process as a compasses, the duodenum at the solar plexus sits as a G in the centre of an anatomical square and compasses!

What else is located at the solar plexus? The third chakra (there's that letter G / number 3 again!). According to chakra anatomy, the message of the third chakra is: *You have the power to choose.* What is the power of choice otherwise known as? Consciousness.

What is consciousness? Your divine spark, your true self, your inner wisdom.

So you see, the G in the centre of the Masonic square and compasses is a loud, blatant message for all who have eyes to see it. It screams at us: *you have a divine spark at your centre.*

To activate your divine spark is to turn inward and connect with your centre. You must find a key to unlock your divine spark and jailbreak it from your material-centric life (dig down into those vaults and find it). Some achieve this through prayer or meditation, others through yoga, music or martial arts. For centuries, the practice of Freemasonry has proven a key to unlocking and activating the divine spark. As esteemed Masonic author Albert Pike wrote: 'Freemasonry is the subjugation of the Human that is in man by the Divine.'[10]

The aim of Freemasonry is to bring under control our material desires to enable the rise of our divine spark, that is, the part of us that is perfect, unblemished and pure, that can never be extinguished and is a divine extension of a higher power. This being the crux of Freemasonry, you understand why so many successful people over the centuries committed a vast amount of their time to the study of Masonic symbolism as a means of turning inward and connecting with their centre to unleash the power of their divine spark.

Masonic author Manly P. Hall wrote that: '…behind these diverse forms there is one connected Life Principle, the spark of God in all living things… this divine spark shines out as brightly from the body of a foe as it does from the dearest friend.'[11]

Masonic ritual makes mention of the divine spark in no uncertain terms. The Third Degree lecture tells us of an 'imperishable part within us' that is our closeness to a Supreme Intelligence and will never die. In fact, this point is so important that the word never is used three times! The imperishable divine spark will 'never, never, never die.'

The divine spark exists in everyone and is triggered by introspection processes. It is your energetic epicentre, and can help improve quality of life. Through processes of unlocking your divine spark, you will balance the energy levels in your body and be better enabled to meet your goals by having a clear image of what you wish to achieve. You will feel more motivated and positive. By having a positive energetic vibration, you will influence the positive energies around you and attract greater positivity to your life.

You can change what is going on around you and how those things are happening by using your energetic vibration. Just get in touch with your true self, the self not limited by the senses, and allow the divine spark to turn you into a better person, who is ready to change his or her life into a better experience.

Activating your divine spark will allow you to reconnect to the force behind all nature and existence, which has no self-concerns and no limitations – a pathway to a non-physical sense far greater than the physical reality that currently holds your divine spark in a very small, limited box just waiting to be opened.

Unleashed!
The cable tow

It is only through enlightenment that we become conscious of our limitations.
— Nikola Tesla

When he first enters a lodge room for initiation, the candidate for Freemasonry is blindfolded. Around his neck is a rope called a cable tow by which he is led in a circuit of the room.

The cable tow is purely Masonic in use, but as with many Masonic symbols it stems from antiquity. Vases unearthed in ancient Mexico show candidates proceeding through a ceremony of initiation while wearing a noosed rope around their necks. Initiates in the religious ceremonies of the Brahmins, Greeks and Druids, wore halters around their necks. In the mystery schools of Ancient Egypt, a candidate wore a chain around his neck as part of the preparation for initiation. As in Freemasonry, the Egyptian initiate wore a blindfold to represent a state of darkness before entering into the light of symbolic rebirth upon the blindfold's removal.

The cable tow's function in ancient initiations stems in part from man's use of ropes to domesticate animals. Ropes were first fashioned to rein in wild beasts and bring them under control. The rope therefore became an early symbol of mastery over brute nature. When the animal was able to control its own behaviour, the rope was no longer necessary. The removal of the rope signified transcendence of the brute self into a higher state of existence in which one experienced self-control and governance from within. Behaviour and actions were no longer influenced by reactions to the external, but were a response to the internal. As the phrase goes, it's what's inside that counts.

So why does the candidate for Freemasonry wear a cable tow around his neck?

Contrary to the belief of conspiracy theorists and anti-Masons, wearing a cable tow is not a form of hazing. The candidate is not dragged around the lodge room like a wild animal on a leash. The cable tow guides the candidate and impresses upon him a lesson to not rush forward in an unprepared state to obtain the secrets of Freemasonry. The candidate should proceed humbly, meekly, cautiously and under instructed guidance. Ideally, this is how we should obtain and apply *all* knowledge – gradually. In other words, don't rush into stuff, especially important stuff. Acquisition of proper education requires baby steps, not bold and unprepared jumps.

The cable tow represents those forces that keep you in a state of ignorance or darkness. To be led by a rope in a state of darkness requires a leap of faith – complete trust – that no harm will befall you and that you will be lead where you need to go. Symbolically, when your blindfold is removed and vision restored, at which point your cable tow is also removed, you will see the world through new eyes restored to light from a state of darkness.

The cable tow binds the initiate to Freemasonry as a newborn is bound to its mother by an umbilical cord. If the lodge is a symbol of man and the universe, and initiation is birth into a true understanding of yourself and your relationship to the universe, then the cable tow is aptly interpreted as an umbilical cord of sorts.

When the doctor cuts the umbilical cord between mother and child, the physical connection severs but the stronger tether of love remains. Likewise, the removal of the cable tow represents a stronger than physical link to Freemasonry and a commitment to self-improvement and higher learning. The force of an outward restraint is replaced by an internal obligation. The new Mason is born into a life where his eyes will be receptive to the teachings that will enable him to transcend his material existence. He is given the ladder by which to climb above his animal nature, whereby he can become more than his external appearance. That is, more than a good head of hair, white teeth, a six-pack of abs and a healthy bank account. He can become his real self – his transcended self – and, as the saying goes, 'do me.'

The cable tow is symbolic of the bind material life puts on the individual. The removal of the cable tow symbolises the removal of that tie to your animalistic self, the Kama principle of theosophy, your basest existence. It is like a dog on a leash. A dog displaying brutish behaviour requires a tether, lest it savages other dogs or randomly humps the legs of passers-by. Through a gradual progression under instructed guidance, the dog learns not to bite, and the leash is removed.

Living in a material world forces you to wear a cable tow. The followers of Zoroaster believe that everyone has a noose round their neck. Upon death, the noose either falls off those who lived a righteous (illuminated) life or drags the evil doers down to hell.

We are, at our basest, controlled by material possessions. The cable tow's removal is symbolic of progression beyond material constraints. The ties that hold you back from achieving higher learning need to be cut for you to reach your higher aspirations. In Masonic ritual, this call to rise above your animal nature, to aim higher, to truly 'do me' is described as aspiring towards 'nobler deeds, for higher thoughts, for greater achievements.'

Your animal nature is your lowest self. Also known as 'brute nature', 'material nature' and 'base nature', your lowest self is the crudest version of you; unrefined, rough, primitive and unaltered by any processing. The lowest self is centred on the ego, which is made up of such components as: pride, guilt, aggression, anger, hate, selfishness, skepticism, conditional love, hostility, jealousy, lust, addictions, elitism, illusion, denial, conformity, boredom, the need for attention and validation, and the lack of realisation of the divinity in oneself. Your lower self is the proverbial 'devil on your shoulder', your inner loser, your inner victim and your inner hater.

You have a choice: succumb to your lowest self and be its puppet, or to kick it to the wayside and aspire to your higher self. Before your symbolic cable tow can be removed, you must understand that you are capable of higher thoughts – of a life beyond the material and physical.

> A man was walking in the grounds of a traveling circus when he passed by the elephant enclosure. He was confused by the fact that these enormous, majestic animals were being held by a small rope tied to their front leg.
>
> 'I don't get it,' the man thought. 'These massive creatures aren't chained and there's no cage to keep them in. They can break loose of that little rope any time they want, but they don't. It doesn't make any sense.'
>
> The man approached a trainer and asked him why the elephants just stood there, tied to the small rope, and didn't attempt to break free.
>
> 'You see,' answered the trainer, 'when the elephants were young and much smaller, we used the exact same size rope to tie them to a pole. It was enough to hold them in place back then so they wouldn't run away. As the elephants grew up they were conditioned to believe that they could not break free. Even now, as big and as strong as they are, they still believe that this small rope holds them to the pole, so they never try to break the restraint and run free.'

Are you similarly held in place by your own small piece of rope?

Have you been trained to believe that you cannot achieve more than that which your material existence dictates?

Do you believe that fast cars, big houses, more sexual partners, and more money in the bank is all there is to life?

The ability to break free from the small rope that tethers you to the material world begins with faith. Faith doesn't mean praying to God. Faith doesn't require religion. Faith is trusting a path of progression whereby you can let go of your animalistic instincts, even though the path cannot always be seen.

> A man who loved rock climbing was scaling a mountain with a safety rope

> tied around his waist. As night began to fall, his visibility diminished until all around him was black. He was just a few feet away from the top of the mountain when he lost his footing and slipped. He fell into the air plummeting towards the ground. Suddenly the rope about his waist fastened and saved him from a grizzly death, but his body still hung in the air.
>
> Panicked, as he could not gauge his position in the darkness, the man screamed out to God for help.
>
> A deep voice boomed from the night sky and God asked him: 'What do you want me to do?'
>
> 'Save me, God,' answered the panicked man.
>
> 'Do you really think I can save you?'
>
> 'Yes,' the man answered. 'I believe you can.'
>
> 'Then cut the rope tied to your waist,' said God.
>
> The man thought about it for a moment but decided to hold the rope instead with all the strength he could muster.
>
> The following morning, when the sun came up, a rescue team found the man dead and frozen, his hands still wrapped around the rope from which hung his body. He was only one foot away from the ground.

There is life beyond our material existence (clinging to the rope) if only we have the faith to follow it. Remember, faith does not necessarily mean religious faith. Faith is defined as: *a strong belief or trust in someone or something*.

Strong belief counts for a lot in accomplishing more in life, however faith without action is useless. Take, for example, the following story:

> A man trapped by floodwaters ravaging the street around him clung desperately to a pole and prayed to God for help.
>
> A woman paddling a surfboard passed by and said, 'Get on my board and I'll paddle us to safety.'
>
> The man refused and said, 'No thank you. My trust is in God. He will save me.'
>
> An hour later, still clinging to the pole as the floodwaters continued to rise, a boy in a rubber dingy passed by and said, 'Hop aboard! I'll row us to safety.'
>
> The man refused and said, 'No thank you. My trust is in God. He will save me.'
>
> The floodwaters continued to rise and were close to consuming the man when a helicopter appeared overhead. A ladder lowered from the helicopter

and a voice shouted to the man, 'Grab the ladder! I will carry you to safety.'

Even though the water was as high as the man's neck, he refused and said, 'No thank you. My trust is in God. He will save me.'

Ten minutes later the man drowned.

Shortly after, he found himself at the Pearly Gates of heaven. Disillusioned at having lost his life, the man said to God, 'Lord, why did you forsake me? I prayed for you to save me and you let me drown.'

God shook His head in disbelief and said to the man, 'I sent you a surf board, a rubber dingy and a helicopter. What else did you want me to do?'

Faith is important but you also need to know when to act and take matters into your own hands. Faith alone will not do the work for you.

The rope of a Masonic cable tow is three separate strands joined as one, symbolic of the three aspects of faith.

The first aspect of faith is intellectual awareness of something. You can't have faith in nothing. Be aware of what you have faith in and be strong in your belief.

The second aspect of faith is conviction of the truthfulness of the information. Don't have blind faith in something because you were born into it. Blind faith in institutional programming drilled into you since birth reduces you to a follower, not a leader. Programmed mechanisms represent a cable tow that restricts your advancement.

The third aspect of faith is in trusting the information. If the ethos of your institutional programming is not improving you intellectually, mentally and spiritually, and does not allow you to transcend your lower nature, it is defaulting on its raison d'être and is a cable tow that needs removing.

The three aspects of faith, represented by the three strands of the cable tow, are further summarised as follows:

1. Awareness of avenues in life that lead to your betterment.
2. Being convinced such avenues are tried and tested.
3. Putting your trust in these avenues to make you a better person.

Faith is not merely blind trust in something. Faith is about believing *in* (1), believing *on* (2) and believing *into* (3) something that will lead your life in an upward direction. It is an intellectual embrace of a means to an end, the goal of which is elevation to a fuller life 'for nobler deeds, for higher thoughts, for greater achievements.'

Let's look at the 1979 film *Being There* starring Freemason Peter Sellers. *Being There* is the story of Chance, a simple, sheltered gardener who becomes an unlikely trusted adviser to a powerful businessman and an insider in Washington politics.

Toward the end of the film, Chance attends millionaire Rand's funeral where the President is giving the eulogy. Chance wanders off from the ceremony to a pond at the foot of a hill below the Rand mansion. After gently uprighting a small pine tree, Chance gazes up at the mansion and walks into the water. Well, he doesn't walk *into* the water, he actually walks *on* the water. A few steps into his walk he pokes at the water with his umbrella showing us that he's not walking on ice or a hidden bridge; he is, in fact, walking on water. At the same time, the President's eulogy is heard with the words, 'life is a state of mind'.

Chance walks on water because his mind possesses no restrictions about what he can and can't do. Symbolically, he has no cable tow holding him back. His intention to walk on water is so pure, his belief so great, that the rules of nature do not exist (material restrictions gone) and Chance acts at will. At the same time, back at the funeral, the Washington power brokers decide upon Chance as the man they wish to become the next President. The entire scene is a metaphor for how one simple man, with pure intentions and no sense of material restriction, can become the most powerful man in the world.

We each need to take a 'Chance' and remove our cable tow.

The cable tow is tied around both the neck and the arm of the candidate for symbolic purposes. The neck symbolises love, as demonstrated in Proverbs 3:3: 'Let love and faithfulness never leave you; bind them around your neck, write them on the tablet of your heart.'

It is with our arms that we perform all actions, thus manifesting our ego. The positioning of the cable tow around the arm and neck tells us that love and faith (the neck) diminishes our ego (the arms) and erases our sole focus on materialism. In this way the symbolic cable tow guides us from the lower plane of materialism to a plane of higher intelligence. The punk of our nature is replaced by the gentleman, and the bitch replaced by the lady. We become one step closer to divinity, which is not in some far away abode out of our reach, but is inside each of us and attainable through various paths of progressive science, of which Freemasonry is one.

Life Application
'Cannot' is an illusion – don't let illusions stand in your way of actually doing something. If you are constantly tethered to a pole, you will only go so far as the rope around your neck permits.

The ability to break free from the small rope that tethers you to the material world begins with faith. Faith doesn't mean praying to God. Faith does not require religion. Faith is trusting that there is a path of progression, to letting go of your animalistic instincts, even though the path cannot always be seen.

The cable tow teaches you to have faith in yourself and to never sell yourself short. This faith is threefold:

Be aware of avenues in life that can lead you to betterment;

Be convinced that these avenues are tried and tested;

Put your trust in these avenues to make you a better person.

There *is* life beyond your material existence. There *is* more to you than your animal nature, your crude, base self. Break the chains! Sever the rope prevents you from seeing more in your life than material possessions and base desires.

The cable tow is tied around your neck and arm. It is with your arms that you perform all actions, thus manifesting your ego. The positioning of the cable tow, therefore, tells you that it is through love and faithfulness (the neck) that the ego (the arms) is diminished and your sole focus on materialism is removed. Removal of your cable tow allows you to climb from the lower plane of materialism to a higher plane of intelligence.

Ask Yourself

- What limits do I place on myself?
- When I really think about them, are the limits I place on myself true limits or false limits?
- If I could sever my cable tow right now, what would I set out to achieve?
- On a scale of 1 to 10, how much of my life is consumed by material possessions and material pursuits?
- On a scale of 1 to 10, how brightly does my divine spark shine?
- Do I knowingly or unknowingly put a cable tow around anyone else's neck and hold them back from greater achievements?
- What do I lack faith in?
- What am I afraid to do that I could embrace instead of fear?

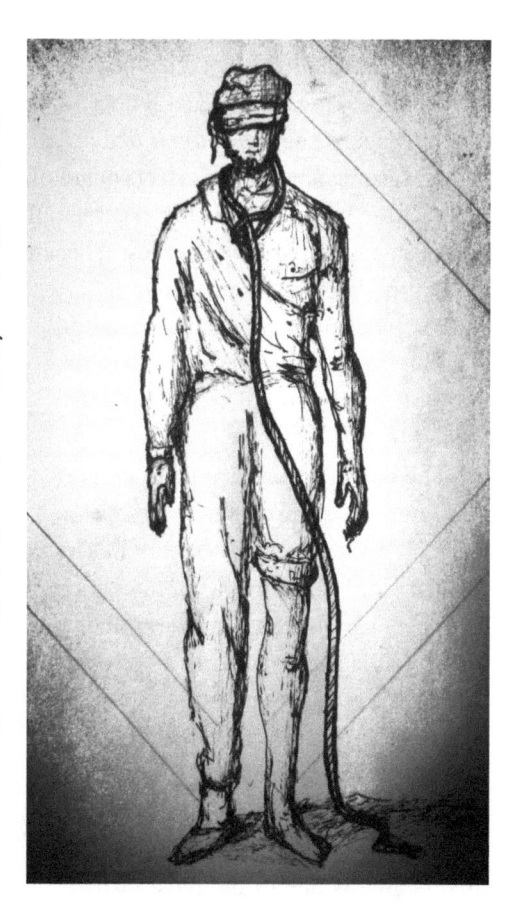

Real men wear aprons
The apron

Imagine that every person in the world is enlightened but you. They are all your teachers, each doing just the right things to help you learn perfect patience, perfect wisdom, perfect compassion.

— Buddha

The first gift a Freemason receives is a white lambskin apron. Referred to as the 'badge of a Mason', the apron is a Freemason's most prized possession and an ancient symbol rich with significance.

A Masonic apron is not the type your mum wears in the kitchen or your dad throws on while cooking a barbecue. It doesn't have fake plastic boobs, pictures of bacon or catchy slogans such as *Chop it like it's hot*.

A Masonic apron is a perfect square of about 14 inches, surmounted by a triangle flap, whose base length is the exact length of one side of the apron and whose apex forms an angle of ninety degrees. It secures around the waist with two strings either tied at the back or, more commonly, with a silver metal clasp in the form of two snakes. The apron covers the waist and genital area of the wearer, the symbolism of which I will soon delve into.

The word 'apron' is a derivative of the English 'napron' (for some reason the 'n' disappeared over time). The French word for apron is *tablie*, which is something that keeps out harmful dirt. A *tablie* also translates as a 'bridge', which is apt symbolically as the new Mason's apron signifies his willingness to bridge the gap between his material self and his higher self.

The apron presentation during the first degree is one of the most visually striking ceremonies in all of Freemasonry. The apron lecture accompanying this presentation is one of unsurpassed beauty in which the recipient is told that the apron is an emblem of innocence and the badge of a Mason; an inspiration for higher thoughts, nobler deeds and greater achievements. A Mason is told to keep his apron spotless, representative of living a spotless life unblemished by impure thoughts or poor actions.

Okay, hold up a minute, you're thinking. *It's a piece of cloth you wear around your waist. That's it! Keep it clean and you're all good, right?*

A Mason's apron is more than a piece of cloth symbolic of keeping himself clean and spotless in his nature. It is an ancient symbol with an origin dating back to the Garden of Eden.

Remember the story of Adam and Eve? Let's visit it again.

God created Adam and then He created Eve. They were both naked and, as Genesis 2:25 tells us, 'they felt no shame.' Fast-forward a few verses to where the serpent persuades Adam and Eve to eat the fruit from the Tree of the Knowledge of Good and Evil. After both eating from the tree, Adam and Even suddenly realise they're naked, as Genesis 3:7 tells us: 'Then the eyes of both of them were opened, and they realised they were naked; so they sewed fig leaves together and made coverings for themselves.'

And there we have the making of the world's first apron born from Adam and Eve's sudden self-consciousness. From then on it was an instinctive part of all races, from savages to the sophisticated, to cover up their genitals and preserve a sense of innocence. Why do you think you're wearing pants now? (At least I hope you are!)

The wearing of aprons is associated throughout history with beings of higher power. Sculptures in Central America show ancient gods wearing aprons. In particular, Tepoxtecatl, the Aztec deity, is depicted wearing a triangular apron over his boy's bits.

Canaanite priests wore white lambskin aprons more than 4000 years ago. Students of the Pythagorean system in Ancient Greece wore garments of white, as did Druidic initiates. The mystery schools of Mithras invested candidates with a white apron, as did the Essenes.[12]

So what does it all mean? Why was a white apron worn by ancient gods, mystery school initiates and high priests? Why are they still worn by Freemasons today?

The colour of the apron holds great significance in understanding its symbolism. Masonic aprons are white, symbolising purity. But there's a deeper meaning to this particular colour.

More than 300 years ago, Sir Isaac Newton performed some cool experiments with light and prisms. He realised that white light was really made up of all the colours combined. The fact that we can't see all these colours at once indicates a weakness in our human eyes. The colour white actually contains millions of colours – we just can't see them all. In fact, we can only see seven of them. This is known as the visible light spectrum. Newton divided the spectrum into seven colours: red, orange, yellow, green, blue, indigo and violet. (Keep the number 7 in mind; we'll come back to it as 7 is a very important number to Freemasons.)

The visible light spectrum is the subdivision of the electromagnetic radiation spectrum that we can see. It is likewise known as the optical spectrum of light. The wavelength, which relates to frequency and energy, determines the colour of the light as we perceive it.[13]

Hold on, what about other colours we can see such as pink or grey?

The visible light spectrum comprises those colours containing only one wavelength, also known as spectral colours or pure colours. Colours such as pink or purple are not contained within the visible light spectrum as their creation occurs through a mixing of multiple wavelengths. Even though the human eye can distinguish about 10 million different colours[14] they are variations of the visible light spectrum.

For those of you with a basic understanding of physics, here are the colours of the visible light spectrum and the wavelength (in nanometers) of each colour:

Red:	625-740
Orange:	590-625
Yellow:	565-590
Green:	520-565
Cyan:	500-520
Blue:	435-500
Violet:	380–435

Thanks for the physics lesson, bud, you're thinking. *Now what the hell does it actually mean?*

No other physical item is ever given to a Freemason except for his apron, which he must wear at all times during lodge. Without an apron, one cannot sit in lodge. Before a lodge opens, the Tyler and Deacons examine each member to make sure they are properly clothed. Any member not wearing an apron must leave the lodge room to clothe himself properly, that is, to put on his apron.

In the apron then we have something visible, worn on the Mason's body, and coloured white. However as physics tells us, within the colour white are all the colours in existence, it's just that our weak human eyes can't see them all. The white apron symbolises the knowledge we have of our material selves, which is all we can learn as an Entered Apprentice (or as a child). Even though all the knowledge of the world and universe is available to us, as a child we can't see it.

The white apron is part of your material make up – literally so. Materially it is nothing more than a piece of cloth traditionally made of lambskin. It is white in colour because your eyes perceive it as such, but it is actually all the colours imaginable. If you confine yourself to your material existence you fail to learn all the other (non-material) knowledge (colours) that can help elevate you to a higher level. If you view the world solely through material eyes, you will only see white for white and not realise that within the white, hidden, some might say *secretly*, is an array of colours (knowledge) waiting to be accessed. This is knowledge that can only be accessed when you transcend above your material nature.

Now that we've established the symbolism of the colour white, let's move onto the meaning behind the number seven.

As stated earlier, a Masonic apron is a square overlaid with a triangular flap. Do you see the number seven?

A square has four sides; a triangle has three sides. This adds up to seven. The ancients considered the number seven a perfect number because it contained a square and a triangle combined: 4 + 3.

The square represents material man; the triangle represents the divine. The triangular flap laid over the square on the Masonic apron symbolises the spiritual within the material. The Master Mason (who has achieved the third degree in Freemasonry) – symbolic of one who has overcome his material state to find his higher, spiritual state – wears his apron with the flap turned down. By doing so, the point of the triangular flap sits dead-centre of the square. This is symbolic of that which is at the very centre of us all – our divine spark.

With this in mind, it should come as no surprise that the Gospel of Matthew (the name Matthew has seven letters), Chapter 7, Verse 7 tells us: 'Ask, and it will be given to you; seek, and you will find; knock, and it will be opened to you.' Note there are 21 words in this verse: 21 equals 7+7+7. Jesus' statement contains the very essence for attaining knowledge and the reason why the candidate for Masonry must first knock three times (7+7+7) on the door of the lodge before admittance.

The teachings of theosophy became popular in the 1800s – also a time for the writing and development of much of the current Masonic ritual. Theosophy is a system of esoteric philosophy concerning, or investigation seeking direct knowledge of, presumed mysteries of being and nature, especially about the nature of divinity.[15]

Founded in 1875 by Helena Petrova Blavatsky (1831 - 1891), the Theosophical Society taught that human beings comprise seven principles, divided into a Higher

Triad and a Lower Quaternary[16], or 3+4 (7). The higher triad lasts forever whereas the lower quaternary lasts just one lifetime. Here is a brief description of the Seven Principles[17]:

THE HIGHER TRIAD

7. ATMA - The Divine Part
Pure eternal spirit. Our higher self.

6. BUDDHI - The Spiritual Part
The spiritual soul through which Atma radiates its light.

5. MANAS - The Intellectual Part
The human soul. The mind. Our thoughts.

THE LOWER QUATERNARY

4. KAMA- The Passional Part
Our sensual nature. Our animal soul. Our lusts, desires, passions.

3. PRANA - The Vital Part
Our life force that keeps us alive.

2. LINGA SHARIRA - The Astral Part
Our astral body. It is through this that Prana flows into and through the physical body.

1. STHULA SHARIRA - The Physical Part
Our actual, physical body made of flesh.

When the mind is elevated towards higher things – beauty, truth, honour, love and greater intellect – the Manas rises closer to the Buddhi. The human soul transcends towards the spiritual soul. This is the pathway of illumination. When the mind settles into the murky depths of sensual things, material desires and selfishness, our animal nature is at work.

What part of the body represents the basest desires in a man?
What part of the body represents your lusts and passions more than any other?

The answer is the genitals.

It is no wonder that the Mason wears his apron around the waist to cover the genitals. This does not mean sex is bad – far from it! The apron covers the genitals to symbolically redirect the negative energy of lust and passions (thinking with the wrong head, is a common expression) up the body to the seat of consciousness, the brain, where this energy is applied to higher learning.

You go through life in a physical body. But inside you, at your centre, is that divine spark you should endeavour to recover. It is the apex of the triangular flap on your symbolic apron, and the part of you made in the image of the Creator. And there's no better geometric figure to symbolise divinity than the triangle.

A triangle is the first shape made by drawing straight lines. This is why ancients venerated the number three – a number still revered today. To Jews, the triangle represents the past, present and future. For the Chinese: heaven, earth and water; the Hindus: creation, preservation and renewal. The three points of the triangle also represent the conscious mind, the subconscious mind and the collective unconscious. The Ancient Egyptian ceremony of initiation led the candidate to a door shaped the same as a Masonic apron: a triangle over a square, symbolising his progression from an earthly, material existence (square) to a spiritual existence of higher learning (triangle).

Just as the Mason keeps a spotless physical apron, you should maintain a spotless symbolic apron. A clean apron indicates a clean conscience. The apron is a reminder to strive for a spotless and pure life, unblemished in thoughts and actions. Cleanliness is next to godliness, and your apron's whiteness symbolises cleanliness of the mind, body and soul.

Attaining pure whiteness, which holds all colours of the universe (all knowledge), is your end goal. Interestingly in the Book of Revelations 2:17, the reward the Lord gives to one who conquers his base self is a white stone: 'To the one who is victorious, I will give some of the hidden manna. I will also give that person a white stone with a new name written on it, known only to the one who receives it.'

The giving of a new name was common practice in the Bible for those who achieved higher learning and elevation of character. Your goal then is to elevate yourself above your animal (material) nature. Wear an apron (not a physical apron, of course, that would look silly sitting on the train to work) to serve as a constant reminder that everything you do in life should help you progress to a higher self.

So what does it mean to rise above your human nature?

Franz Hartmann MD details it eloquently: 'If we follow our instincts, we act naturally – that is to say, according to the demands of our animal nature; but if we resist natural impulses by the power of will and reason, we employ powers belonging to a higher order of Nature. If we avoid evil on account of the evil consequences which it would cause to ourselves, we act naturally; but if we avoid it on account of an inherent love for the good, we act on a plane above our animal nature.'[18]

Let's use the example of a parent disciplining their child.

A young boy hits his sister and is scolded by his mother who grounds him. In trying to further impart the message of her disciplinary action, she asks her son, 'Why should you never hit your sister again?'

The young son answers, 'Because if I do, you will get angry and ground me.'

The mother acknowledges this as the correct response, but in doing so she does not properly discipline and educate her son. He may not hit his sister again, but as Hartmann explains, he does so to 'avoid evil on account of the evil consequences which it would cause'. It is natural to act as such but does not elevate the young boy's actions above his animal nature.

A better response from the mother is, 'you shouldn't hit your sister again, not because you're scared of me punishing you but because you love your sister and, out of love for her, you never wish to harm her.' Thus, as Hartmann says, the young boy avoids the evil action 'on account of an inherent love for the good' and acts on a plane above his animal nature.

Act with kindness out of love for your fellow human beings, not through fear of punishment. Do unto others, as you would have them do unto you. This is the Golden Rule, the Universal Law, with which you need to comply if you are to elevate yourself above your animal nature and transcend.

What is transcendence?

Transcendence is true freedom and what separates us from animals. It is our remarkable human capacity to climb above programmed responses to outer variables and discover causality inside. Transcendence is the freed awareness which has arrived at such level of improvement that it can see itself as the reason and is no longer a slave to the conditioning of society and environment.

Transcendence reveals your real self. Not the self characterised by associations with your outer self (how you look, your job, your marriage, your hobbies, your lusts, your material desires). It is the union between the awareness and the vitality, the dynamic rule that enlivens you, and is not simply one of several adapted responses to the external influences in your life, such as the young boy no longer hitting his sister for fear of being grounded.

Most people characterise themselves in connection to their external selves. This is human nature. We perceive ourselves as being what we see in the mirror and nothing more. Our actual extraordinary nature recognises ourselves as totally free from such outer definitions.

Don't curl into a dark corner and let society control your thoughts, actions and education. Develop your internal self. Be like a seed.

Within the seed is the means to grow into a mighty tree. Even the largest redwood begins as a modest seed. However, changing from seed to tree does not happen overnight. A seed becomes a shoot, a shoot becomes a sapling, and a sapling becomes a tree. The tree is firmly rooted in the earth and is thus connected to all nature.

As the tree receives nourishment from the earth, so your spirit receives nourishment from the universe and is connected to all energy. It is your divine spark, represented by the apex of the triangle in the centre of your symbolic apron. This is how a Master Mason (an enlightened adult) wears his apron – with the triangular flap turned down. An Entered Apprentice (a child) wears his apron with the flap turned up whereby the apex of the triangle sits above the square, symbolising the divine spark above the physical self.[19]

You should aspire to attain the education necessary to bring the apex of the triangle – the divine spark – to the centre of your self, thus forming the shape of the Master's apron. Remember, the Master is symbolic of one who has overcome his animal, crude, base nature to realise the divine spark or higher nature within himself.

Don't let your animal side dictate your life. Don't sit on the branch because it's safe. Set your mind to the task of earnest self-improvement through diligent work. You emerge from darkness by letting white light shine upon you. Always wear an apron symbolic of 'purity of life and rectitude of conduct, a never-ending argument for nobler deeds, for higher thoughts, for greater achievements.'

Life Application

A Mason's apron is to remain spotless at all times. Your symbolic apron must also remain spotless. The knowledge you acquire to elevate your mental and spiritual nature should be pure and true. Misinformation and education of an evil nature keeps you attached to the base nature you must try to transcend.

To attain a higher self should be your life's aim. The wearing of a symbolic white apron serves as a constant reminder that everything you do in life should serve one purpose – the attainment of your higher self.

Physics tells us that the colour white contains all colours in existence but our weak human eyes can't see them all. The white apron therefore symbolises the knowledge you have of your material self but within which is the knowledge of the universe. Work toward attaining this knowledge. White is only white to those who see the world through material eyes. If you confine yourself to a material existence, you will fail to learn about all the other knowledge that elevates you to a higher level. A clean apron indicates a clean conscience. The apron is a reminder to strive toward a spotless and pure life of unblemished thoughts and actions.

Don't let your animal side dictate your life. Don't stay stagnant and wrap yourself in cotton wool because it's safe. Set your mind to the task of earnest self-improvement through diligent work.

At the centre of your symbolic apron, at your core, is a divine spark. This is the god-like part in you. It is pure, spotless and brilliant, but trapped within the walls of your animal nature. Remember, you are fearlessly and wonderfully made. There is only one of you for all time! Wear your symbolic apron to prevent soiling your soul and keep your divine spark burning bright. Do not stain your character, nor let your education and aspirations become muddied by insecurities or capitulation to what society deems you should, and should not, do in life.

Ask Yourself
- Is my conscience clean or does a bad conscience keep me up at night?
- How can I clean the blemishes on my conscience?
- Do I choose social acceptance over my heart's desire?
- Am I choosing to stay in my comfort zone over adventure?
- Am I allowing new knowledge into my life?
- What is a subject I would like to learn more about?
- What ignites my brain?
- Am I deceiving myself by limiting my thoughts?
- When I don't limit myself by preconceived (built in) thoughts, what possibilities open up for me?

It's your time
The 24-inch gauge

Every morning you are handed 24 golden hours.
They are one of the few things in this world that you get free of charge.
If you had all the money in the world, you couldn't buy an extra hour.
What will you do with this priceless treasure?

—Anonymous

In the three degrees of Freemasonry[20], the Mason is symbolically given a different set of builder's tools, known as working tools. Freemasons are taught that the speculative use of these tools is to build the self; more specifically to build the soul, referred to as 'that house not made with hands.'

A Freemason builds his mind and spirit, just as a martial artist or a bodybuilder builds his body. Think of Freemasonry as martial arts for the mind and soul, strengthening the psychical state, not the physical body. The internal and not the external qualifications of a man is what Freemasonry regards and strengthens.

The first working tool presented to a Freemason is the 24-inch gauge, made of three sections of equal eight-inch length and used operatively by builders to measure their work.

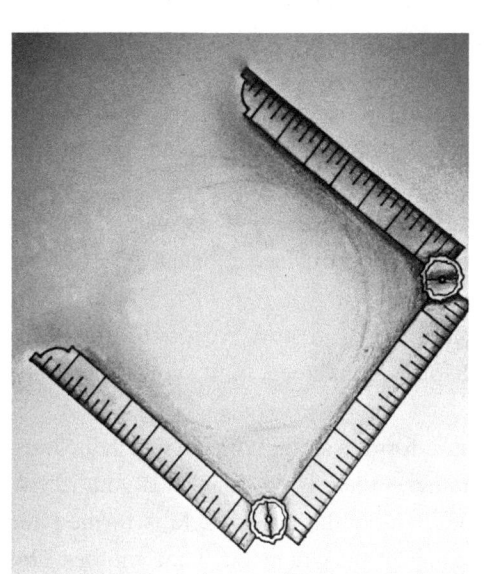

If Freemasons are taught to use the working tools for the symbolic building of their non-physical self, what does the 24-inch gauge symbolically teach and how can this teaching be applied to your everyday life?

The chief lesson of the 24-inch gauge deals with time and how to use this most precious commodity. The 24-inch gauge represents the 24 hours in a day. Masons are taught that the day should be divided into three equal parts: eight hours for the service of God and a distressed worthy brother; eight hours for work; and eight hours for refreshment and sleep.

You may be rolling your eyes after reading the above paragraph and wondering, *how on earth can I break up all the activities I do each day into these three specific parts? Eight hours for the service of God? Eight hours only for eating AND sleeping? Come on!*

You're right! Unless you're a Tibetan Sherpa or a hermit living in a cave beneath a waterfall, it's pretty much impossible to divide your time equally into these three parts. But what's important is the lesson, not a verbatim adherence to the wording.

The 24-inch gauge teaches that time is one of, if not *the* most valuable commodity in your life. Value time above all material riches. It cannot be bought but is often spent lightly and squandered. That the first tool presented to the newly made Mason is one which teaches the use of time, is indicative of time's importance. Before you can achieve anything in life, you must learn how to use your time.

Imagine, for a moment, a magic bank that at the stroke of midnight deposits £864,000 into your account, being £10 for every second in the upcoming 24-hour day. You can use this money as you wish, but at the end of the day when the clock strikes 11:59:59, your bank account is completely erased with no carry over to the following day.

What would you do if you had such a bank account? You'd try to spend every pound! This is how time works.

Every hour you don't spend wisely is another £36,000 your account writes off as a loss. You can't draw against tomorrow; you can't put more money into the account and you can't put it into a retirement package to use later in life. You must use your money now and spend it to the best of your abilities, otherwise it's gone forever.

The 24-inch gauge teaches another lesson, that of balance. The newly made Mason is instructed to divide the day equally into three parts of 8 hours each, thus promoting balance in a 24-hour period.

Without balance, life becomes haphazard. Without balance, focus is lost. Without balance, stability is absent. One pillar cannot hold a structure in balance, just as one leg cannot hold a body in balance.

Balance is essential in all we do, particularly in how we divide our time. The 24-inch gauge is a perfect tool for displaying balance, both symbolically and operatively.

When the 24-inch gauge is flattened out, it forms a straight line in which the three sections of the gauge do not touch one another – there is no balance. If you lift two legs of the gauge and join them at an apex, an equilateral triangle is formed and perfect balance achieved in which all three legs of the gauge touch one another. This perfect balance is achieved only when the legs are set to equal proportion with one another.

The equilateral triangle is a symbol worth further investigation. Masonic author, Albert Pike, placed great importance on the triangle and its esoteric meaning. In his book *Morals and Dogma,* Pike asserts that Geometry, as one of the Seven Liberal Arts and Sciences[21], is a misnomer and that the more applicable science to the Freemason would be trigonometry – the study of triangles.[22]

Interestingly, the compasses used to form the famous square and compasses logo of Freemasonry, are always opened to an angle of 60° – or one-third of an equilateral triangle. Sixty degrees also equates to one-third of a 24-inch gauge, which lies at 180° when flattened out.

The equilateral triangle is the oldest symbol in the world. It is no coincidence that the first working tool the Mason receives forms such an age-old and much-revered emblem. The ancients revered the equilateral triangle as a symbol of perfection and complete balance:

- the balance of the divine trinity – Father, Son, Holy Spirit;
- the balance of time – past, present and future;
- the balance of self – mind, body and spirit;
- the balance of nature – animal, mineral and vegetable.

The use of two equilateral triangles with one point up (to the spiritual) and one point down (to the earthly) forms the symbol of a hexagram, which represents the balance between man and his higher self, between heaven and earth, the harmony of opposites, representative of the Hermetic maxim: as above, so below. *Quod est inferius est sicut quod est superius, et quod est superius est sicut quod est inferius.* That which happens on the physical level also happens on the psychical level. What happens in your mind (above) is reflected in your body and environment (below). What you think, you become.

Live your life as an ascent into the purity of perfection that is the principal state of us all. This goal requires the curbing of passions and lusts, and the establishment of a state of inner balance and harmony. Try a little every day to dedicate yourself to the perfection of your personality and the creation of balance, whereby the three arms of your 24-inch gauge connect as one, equal in all its sides.

Life is a pursuit of balance. Balance is represented throughout Masonry by the duality of various symbols: the two pillars; the Senior and Junior Wardens; the sun and the moon; the black and white tiles on the mosaic pavement; the Senior and Junior Deacons; the inner and outer door.

Most religions and ancient schools of teaching, particularly those of Eastern origin, emphasise the essential need for balance in life. In Buddhism there is the principle of the 'Middle Way'; in Confucianism the 'Doctrine of the Mean'; in Taoism there is balance between yin and yang; and in Hinduism the concept of balancing the chakras.

The first thing you should learn to balance is time. If you feel run off your feet at work and aren't getting enough sleep at night, your life will be out of balance – symbolically, the legs of your 24-inch gauge will not meet proportionately, thus failing to form an equilateral triangle.

Likewise, if you neglect your profession and over-excess in refreshment, you may soon find yourself out of a job and without an income, which in turn will cripple your ability to enjoy life because, again, your 24-inch gauge is out of proportion.

Take the time to help *a worthy, distressed brother* – someone worthy of your help – whether by carrying an elderly neighbour's shopping bags or helping your children with their homework. The Law of the Universe dictates that if you lead a selfish life, you will not receive a helping hand when one is needed.

Spending time *for the service of God* is a phrase, which upon first reading, may ruffle the feathers of someone who does not believe in God. Even someone who does believe in God may be thinking, *there's no way I'm going to spend eight hours a day praying to God!* To interpret the Masonic instruction in this way is to miss the true meaning of the lesson.

'For service to God' alludes to time spent doing something pleasing to a higher power, let's say, your higher self, your spirit, guardian angels, or your conscience. This involves any activity done truly and done well, so long as it does not waste precious time.

Spending time with friends at home or out clubbing may not seem like 'service to God' but if such time is well spent, with laughter, good conversation, appreciation and acceptance, then it pleases your higher self. Time spent studying a new subject, such as partaking in an online course or night school to further your knowledge of the world and feed your brain, is time well spent and thus pleasing to your higher self. Time spent reading to your child, talking to your partner about their day, helping a charity or even working out at the gym to stay in shape is time well spent and pleasing to your higher self. Find balance every day and spend each minute wisely and without waste.

Working out at the gym for two hours while your wife toils with the kids is not time well spent. Spending money at a club, while your husband tries to balance the cheque-book because of cutbacks at work, is not time well spent.

That the founders of Freemasonry considered time management so important as to delegate the first working tool to its subject speaks volumes for the forward thinking of these wise men. They knew, as we do now, that the highest achievers all have one thing in common – they manage their time exceptionally well.

The use of the 24-inch gauge tells us that time management is not a product of modern society. Time management may be big business today, but it has always been an important part of self-improvement. Time management includes the development of routine. The lesson of the 24-inch gauge breaks the day into three equal parts, thus providing instruction on organising your day in such a way as to allocate specific time for specific activities. Such organisation develops routine and ensures you do not live each day haphazardly.

The importance of establishing routine is based on the science of the circadian rhythm, which is set by your body's internal clocks, known as biological clocks. The biological clocks that control circadian rhythm are groupings of interacting molecules in cells throughout the body. A 'master clock' in the brain coordinates all the body clocks to be in synch.[23]

Your master clock controls your circadian rhythm set to a 24-hour cycle. It regulates your body's sleep and metabolism, and its chemical and hormonal production. This internal clock is integral to your well-being. The incorrect setting of your body's internal clock results in a negative impact on your ability to function. Jet-lag produces such an experience. Traveling great distances between various time zones throws your internal clock out of order and affects your sleep and energy levels. Throwing out your internal clock for longer periods of time may cause more serious damage including an increased risk of cancer and cardiovascular disease. Abnormal circadian rhythms are associated with obesity, diabetes, depression, bipolar disorder, and seasonal affective disorder.[24]

Your circadian clock is located in the suprachiasmatic nucleus or nuclei (SCN), situated in the hypothalamus region of the brain directly above the optic chiasm where the optic nerves partially cross.[25] The two hemispheres of the brain contain one suprachiasmatic nucleus each, consisting of about 20,000 neurons. It is a tiny gathering of neurons responsible for one of the body's most important jobs. They are, effectively, the body's timekeepers, responsible for regulating hormone production, glucose and insulin levels, sleeping patterns, alertness, brain wave activity, feeding patterns, urine production, and cell regeneration.[26]

Zeitgebers affect your circadian clock. From the German for 'time giver', zeitgebers are external or environmental cues that synchronise your biological rhythms to the Earth's light and dark cycle. Examples of zeitgebers include light, exercise, temperature, social interactions, manipulation through drugs, and eating/drinking patterns.[27] The Earth's cycle of light and darkness is the most important of these zeitgebers and transmits to the suprachiasmatic nuclei through the eyes, allowing the circadian clock to reset itself each day according to the Earth's 24-hour rotation cycle.[28]

Circadian rhythms determine sleep patterns. The suprachiasmatic nuclei control melatonin production, a hormone that makes you sleep. Melatonin is produced by the pineal gland, a small pinecone shaped gland in the centre of the brain. Information on the light/dark cycles reaches the suprachiasmatic nuclei from the ganglion cells of the eyes (see later chapters on the All-Seeing Eye and Light). At dusk when light diminishes, the suprachiasmatic nuclei instructs the brain to develop more melatonin – known as the hormone of darkness – to induce drowsiness in diurnal animals such as humans, and activity in nocturnal animals such as red eye tree frogs, bats, owls and possums.

The developers of the symbolic 24-inch gauge may or may not have known of the science of circadian rhythm but were well aware that without adequate time allocated to the body's needs – without routine – the physical self deteriorates. Likewise, without allocation of time for psychical needs, the higher self enters into a state of decline.

The 24-inch gauge should serve as a wake-up call to be introspective, and consider how you use your time.

Are you really spending time with your kids or merely humouring them when they want to learn and play?

Are you honestly spending quality time with your partner while sitting on a chair across the room watching television?

Are you genuinely performing your best at work while spending time on Facebook or taking a cigarette break?

Do you ever contemplate all the privileges and gifts you've received and wonder if there is a higher power at work to which you should give thanks?

Time is precious. It is a constantly diminishing commodity. Never take it for granted. Never expect there to be another minute, another hour or another day. Make the most of the now and be in the present, which is the only place you can ever be. As author C.S. Lewis wrote: 'The future is something which everyone reaches at the rate of sixty minutes an hour, whatever he does, whoever he is.'

You can't speed up time and you can't slow it down, all you can do is learn to use time effectively so that it serves you and doesn't keep you a prisoner of its never-ending progress (in which case you would serve time!)

The only time that exists is *your* time. You can use your time to help others – a distressed worthy brother – but you can never spend someone else's time for them. Right now, reading this book, you are experiencing *your* time, which is the only time you can ever experience. Your wife may be getting her nails done, your husband may be watching the football, your child may be playing with their toys – that is *their* time. You can be a part of their time but you can never spend their time for them. There is a proverb, which says that killing time is not murder, it is suicide. To waste time is to harm yourself and squander the most precious commodity you've been given.

Heed the words of the anonymous author who wrote of the 24-inch gauge and its lessons: 'Time - man's greatest mystery, bitterest enemy, truest friend! Its care, conservation, employment, is the secret of the twenty-four inch gauge.'

Life Application

Time is a valuable commodity. Don't waste it! Realise that the past and the future are illusions, and the only time you can truly act, react, and think within, is the present.

Make the most of your time to better your life and the lives of those around you. Be organised, be efficient and be ritualistic in your use of time. Ritual is part of your human make up. Without ritual, you become disorganised, which leads to procrastination and frustration.

All things are possible given time. Though we focus on the moment, we must learn to divide these moments for service to our profession, our family, our friends, our health and to the acknowledgement of a higher intelligence. Time consumed by material things limits you to material advancement only.

Time is valued above all material riches yet it cannot be bought, and it should not be spent lightly nor squandered.

Nothing can be done in life without making the time to do it. Before you can achieve anything, you must learn how to use time effectively through balance. A balanced life is imperative for personal progression.

Without balance, life becomes haphazard. Without balance, focus is lost. Without balance, stability is absent. One pillar cannot hold a structure in balance, just as one leg cannot hold a body in balance.

The 24-inch gauge breaks the day into three equal parts of eight hours each. This is not an admonition to adhere to these exact three sectionals but rather to organise your day in such a way that you have specific time allocated for specific activities, and do not live each day haphazardly.

Ask Yourself
- Am I using this time – right now – the best I can?
- Am I serving my higher self in any way?
- Do I have a routine in my daily life that best serves my time?

- Am I utilising my time in such a way as to see progression in my daily life in all things I hope to achieve?
- Am I prioritising my time and achieving each priority?
- Have I set priorities according to importance, not urgency?
- Do I have a daily schedule, a monthly schedule and a yearly schedule of what I would like to achieve within those time frames?
- Can I do something productive while waiting?
- Am I making time for the important people in my life? (partner, child, mother, father, etc.)
- Would my higher self be happy with how I am using my time right now?

Keep chipping away
The common gavel

Men are more easily governed through their vices than through their virtues.
— Napoleon Bonaparte

The common gavel is one of the three working tools given the Freemason in the Entered Apprentice Degree, along with the 24-inch gauge and the chisel.

Judges use a gavel to bring order to a courtroom. Auctioneers rap a gavel as the acceptance of a final bid. American politicians in both the House of Representatives and the Senate wield a gavel while debating how the country should be run.

Famously in 1954, Vice President Richard Nixon broke the Senate's gavel during a heated late-night debate on nuclear energy. The ivory gavel, fitted with iron plates on both ends in 1952 to prevent deterioration, had been in use since 1789! Bad luck was on Tricky Dicky's side from the start.

Like most Masonic symbols, the gavel is a simple tool with a seemingly simple use: it calls people to order. In the hands of the Master of the lodge, the gavel calls the lodge and its various officers to labour or refreshment. One rap of the gavel calls a particular officer to stand; two raps calls for all officers to rise; three raps calls for the entire lodge (officers and non-officers) to rise. One further rap calls for the lodge to sit. This is the operative use of the gavel within a Masonic lodge. However, every Masonic tool has both an operative and speculative usage, that is, each tool teaches a lesson in self-improvement.

In operative use, the common gavel breaks off the corners of rough stones, to better fit them for the builder's purpose. Speculatively, the gavel divests our hearts and consciences of all the vices and superfluities of life. In other words, the gavel teaches us to chip away at the rough edges of our personal makeup.

Imagine yourself as a building under construction in which each brick is part of your overall structure. These individual building blocks, which create your whole, represent every aspect of your being – material (body), mental (mind) and spiritual (soul). Each block is perfectly shaped with precise angles, perfect horizontals and aligned perpendiculars to fit seamlessly into the overall structure. An incorrectly prepared block, wrongly shaped, rough-edged or poorly angled, does not meet the architect's requirements. In this instance, the architect is God, the universe, the creating force, nature, or whatever your perception of the architect of life. A block unable to fit into the structure due to rough edges renders the building incomplete. A person who appears to have a 'few screws loose' really has a few imperfect blocks in their building.

The pyramids of ancient Egypt offer examples of structures built with a distinct plan and the utmost precision – the work of an amazing architect. One of the largest man-made structures, the Great Pyramid at Giza measures at its sides: 230.25 meters North; 230.25 meters South; 230.39 meters East; 230.36 meters West.[29] The difference of only 14 centimeters between its shortest and longest sides is minuscule in a structure of such tremendous size![30]

The faces of the pyramid align almost perfectly to its cardinal points with an average error around three minutes of an arc (a deviation from true of less than 0.015 per cent), which is mind-boggling by today's construction standards let alone for a structure built over 4500 years ago. Also consider that the pyramid contains more than two million blocks, all precisely shaped, each weighing between 2.5 and 15 tons and elevated 100 feet or higher. Consider too that the apex of the pyramid sits exactly over the centre of the base.[31] As someone who struggles to build a coffee table from Ikea, the precision of the pyramids is truly astounding.

The pyramids of ancient Egypt symbolise perfection through the precise design, measurement, and fashioning of its individual blocks. As a builder of your self, you too should aspire to construct with precision and perfection. To achieve perfection, fit your building with blocks precisely rendered, devoid of rough edges and individually crafted. Treat each block as a separate piece of the building fitted to complete the whole.

The new Mason receives a 24-inch gauge, chisel and common gavel as his first three working tools. The writers of Masonic ritual knew that a man should waste no time (24-inch gauge) getting an education (chisel) and breaking off the rough corners of his character (common gavel) before the will to do so subsides. There's no dilly-dallying around in character building. We're handed a bunch of tools, an apron to carry them in, and told to punch our time card and go to work from the moment we're made an Entered Apprentice, symbolically the moment we emerge from childhood into adolescence.

According to Masonic writings, the roughness that requires smoothing are all the 'vices and superfluities' of life.

Sounds a little ambiguous, doesn't it? Try telling a builder to 'smooth out the superfluities' and he's likely to flip you off and go for a smoke break. Let's break down exactly what is meant by 'vices' and 'superfluities'.

The word vice derives from the Latin *vitium* meaning fault, flaw, crime or weakness. Vice is immoral behaviour, an evil habit or practice, a particular form of depravity or a fault, defect or shortcoming. Indeed the word 'shortcoming' is the best definition of vice for our current purposes.

As products of our environment in a flawed society, shortcomings inevitably enter our lives. Shortcomings are flaws in our thoughts and actions. Using the allegory of building blocks in the construction of ourselves, any flawed block causes the structure to fail. To have a shortcoming – a flaw – is to have a rough edge on a building block of life. To complete the building, smooth all rough edges to fit seamlessly into the structure.

Lying, cheating, stealing, greed and selfishness are vices possessed by most. Other vices include smoking, alcoholism, and gambling, sexual depravity and food addiction. The seven deadly sins, known as the capital vices, are: wrath, greed, sloth, envy, pride, lust and gluttony.

Meh, it's out of my control, you're thinking. *Vices are part of human nature; we can never get rid of them. It's just the way it is!*

The gavel tells you that it is possible through time to smooth your rough edges.

An operative builder chips away at the rough edges of rocks through a time-consuming process. Likewise, the gavel symbolically teaches that attaining smoothness in your building blocks by divesting your heart and conscience of all the vices is not achieved overnight but through time. Remember, you have a gavel, not a reciprocating saw. The gavel breaks off rough stone one chip at a time. With dedicated usage, the gavel *will* eventually smooth out the stone, but the process requires dedication, patience, and persistence. The gavel works by your hand only – your own willpower and action. It doesn't plug into a power socket for quick and easy results.

What about the word 'superfluities'?

The Merriam-Webster dictionary defines superfluity as: *excess, oversupply; something unnecessary or superfluous; immoderate and especially luxurious living, habits or desires.*

The Chinese philosopher[32], Xun Zi (300-230BCE) said: 'Pride and excess bring disaster for man.' In a capitalist world of increasing materialism it is easy to be sucked into a life of excess. We crave more money; a larger house; a faster car; more food than we require for sustenance; more alcohol than is necessary for refreshment; a fast track to fortune through gambling; sexual encounters with multiple partners; the newest shoes despite the pairs already in our closet; and the latest fashion trends despite the racks of clothing we never wear.

All ancient sages taught the importance of divesting superfluities, including Mahavira (599 BCE - 527 BCE), the founder of Jainism, an Indian religion which teaches non-violence, equality, and spiritual independence. Born into a royal family with all the riches and excesses of life at his fingertips, Mahavira abandoned the comforts of royal life at the age of thirty and traveled far and wide teaching a philosophy of equality. His message was simple: the pursuit of pleasure is an endless game. The mind should be trained to curb individual cravings and passions.

The same teaching is at the heart of Freemasonry. One of the greatest duties of a Mason is to 'subdue' his passions. Note that Freemasonry uses the word 'subdue' rather than the word 'suppress'. The Merriam-Webster dictionary defines the word 'subdue' as *to achieve a victory over.* The definition of 'suppress' is *to hold back the normal growth of and to put a stop to.*

Freemasonry teaches one to take control of their passions, not to stop to them altogether. Passions, both positive and negative, are part of human make-up. Do not deny your nature. A true master keeps his passions in check; he does not stamp them out completely.

Mastership over passions is a common theme in the Sacred Law of most religions.

> Manifest plainness,
> Embrace simplicity,
> Reduce selfishness,
> Have few desires.
> – *Buddhism. Samyutta Nikaya xlvii.37*

If out of the three hundred songs I had to take one phrase to cover all my teachings, I would say, 'Let there be no evil in your thoughts'.
– *Confucianism. Analects 2.2*

Realising that pleasure and pain are personal affairs, one should subjugate his mind and senses.
– *Jainism. Acarangasutra 2.78*

Beloved, I beseech you ... to abstain from the passions of the flesh that wage war against your soul.
– *Christianity, 1 Peter 2.11*

Is he who relies on a clear proof from his Lord like those for whom the evil that they do seems pleasing while they follow their own lusts?
– *Islam. Qur'an 47.14*

That man is disciplined and happy:
Who can prevail over the turmoil
that springs from desire and anger,
here on earth, before he leaves his body.
– *Hinduism. Bhagavad Gita 5.23*

A man should always incite the good impulse in his soul to fight against the evil impulse. If he subdues it, well and good; if not, let him study Torah ... If [by that] he subdues it, well and good; if not, let him pray upon his bed.
– *Judaism. Talmud, Berakot 5a*

Wipe out the delusions of the will, undo the snares of the heart, rid yourself of the entanglements to virtue; open up the roadblocks in the way. Eminence and wealth, recognition and authority, fame and profit – these six are the delusions of the will. Appearances and carriage, complexion and features, temperament and attitude – these six are the snares of the heart. Loathing and desire, joy and anger, grief and happiness – these six are the entanglements of virtue. Rejecting and accepting, taking and giving, knowledge and ability – these six are the roadblocks of the Way. When these four sixes no longer seethe within the breast, then you will achieve uprightness; being upright, you will be still; being still, you will be enlightened; being enlightened, you will be empty; and being empty, you will do nothing, and yet there will be nothing that is not

done.
— *Taoism. Chuang Tzu 23*

The gavel chips away at the roughness of your personal building blocks. You are not given a lump of clay or a bucket of cement and told to build blocks from scratch. Perfect blocks are already within you. The divestment of vices and superfluities is within your means if you are willing to do the work. Like the great artist Michelangelo said: 'Every block of stone has a statue inside it, and it is the task of the sculptor to discover it.' Just as Michelangelo saw the angel in the marble and carved until he set it free, so perfection is inside you if you chip away your rough exterior.

Whenever you are confronted with vices and superfluities in life – that extra slice of cake, the temptation to throw your hard-earned money on the roulette table – take hold of your symbolic gavel and chip away at these shortcomings. Knock them off and smooth them out!

Note that the working tool is a 'common' gavel and not simply a gavel. The Master's gavel is an instrument of authority, and symbolically the Master has attained authority over his vices and superfluities. The 'common' gavel is available to everyone to gain control over vices and superfluities. It is better known by its true name – willpower.

Life Application
The gavel of Freemasonry is called a 'common' gavel because it is common to everyone. As a tool common to all and not just in the hands of a few, it teaches that the ability to smooth out your character and chip away at the rough edges of your personality – a major undertaking upon initial contemplation – is in your hands. You possess the means of refinement if you are willing to do the work. A gavel does not lift itself.

The common gavel teaches you to smooth out the vices and superfluities of life. Many see such vices as an inevitable part of life, but succumbing to vices is a *choice* you make. You can *choose* to lie or tell the truth; *choose* to be prideful or humble; *choose* to cheat or play by the rules.

The common gavel acts as a constant reminder to not let vices and superfluities dictate your life and blemish your character. Choose to chip off these rough parts of your personal make-up so you don't become a person people define by your vices. Let no one say of you, 'He's a cheater' or 'She's full of herself' or 'He's selfish and greedy.'

The common gavel is willpower. It is a hand-held tool you must wield into action

– it will not wield itself. It smooths out rough edges one chip at a time through a time-consuming process without shortcuts.

Ask Yourself
- What vices are prevalent in my life?
- Do I have any shortcomings that give a rough edge to my personal building blocks?
- Is what I am doing today getting me closer to where I want to be tomorrow?
- Are my thoughts hurting or healing?
- What are the rough edges of my nature?
- What is the roughest edge of my personality?
- Did I attempt to 'chip away' at any of my shortcomings today?
- What is the most obvious shortcoming in my life I can 'chip away' at?
- Really, truly, is this the best person I can be?

What's the point?
The point within a circle

Happiness resides not in possessions and not in gold, happiness dwells in the soul.
—Democritus

In every Masonic lodge is found a picture of a dot in the centre of a circle between two perpendicular, parallel lines. Known as the Point within a Circle, it is one of the most written-about symbols in all of Freemasonry.

The symbol of the Point within a Circle features prominently on the first degree tracing board. Known as a trestle board, the Masonic tracing board emanates from an operative origin. In medieval stonemason guilds, the master builder drew his daily designs on a tracing board for the workmen to follow. Not unlike the plans of a modern architect, the master drew his tracing board on whatever material was available at the time. Most commonly, he drew the tracing board on the floor so it could be erased at night to protect the design specifications from unqualified eyes.

Masonic tracing boards contain symbols embedded into detailed pictures. To the non-Mason, these pictures appear as colourful illustrations with random scatterings of such symbols as pillars, compasses, ladders, staircases, skulls and crossbones, wheat, corn, rivers and more. But to the Freemason, the tracing boards are detailed picture books that relay easily recognisable moral and spiritual messages on how to live and how to die. Knowledge of symbols gives the key to unlocking their meaning. Once you know the symbols, the messages of the tracing boards hit you like the discovery of the hidden image in a Magic Eye book. You need not be Alan Turing to crack the code of Masonic symbols. But like Turing, who spent years at Bletchley Park breaking the German Enigma code, the study of symbolism is a pursuit that takes time and patience.

The Point within a Circle may look like something drawn by a ten year old with a ruler and protractor, but this seemingly simple symbol contains a blue print of who you are. In brief, the Point within a Circle is the architect's drawing for the building of a person.

Freemasonry teaches that the point represents the individual and the circle represents the boundary line of one's duty to God and his fellow man. Masons are taught that so long as a man keeps his passions so circumscribed, he cannot err.

Nice little lesson, isn't it? But it's not enough. Masonic symbols are like onions – you peel away one layer and there's another layer underneath. The lesson taught in the ritual about circumscribing your passions is important, but it is not the centre of the onion. It's Turing cracking only one letter of the Enigma encryption.

Masonic author Albert Mackey wrote that the Point within a Circle represents regeneration and stems from ancient phallus worship – the point representing the phallus, the circle representing the female reproductive organs. Taking the symbolism further, Mackey wrote that the point represents the sun (male) and the circle the universe (female) which is 'invigorated and fertilised by his regenerative rays'.[33]

When I look at the Point within a Circle, I don't see a penis inside a vagina, nor do I associate it with Ancient Egyptian phallus worship.

I'm not saying Mackey is wrong in his interpretation of the symbol. Interpretation is a matter of opinion derived from one's experience. Mackey meditated on the symbol and interpreted it as symbolic of the male and female aspects of regeneration. One of the true joys of free thinking is to meditate on symbols and discover what each means to you. A symbol has different meanings to different people, and that's okay!

Before we examine the circle, let's look at the dot, or point, at the circle's centre.

A point is the beginning, starting place or origin of any design. No shape, design or plan is drawn without a starting point. Even the great masterpieces such as Botticelli's *The Birth of Venus* or Monet's *Woman with a Parasol* began as a dot on a canvas.

To start a drawing, one places a writing instrument on a surface, thus creating a starting point from which the rest of the picture emanates. This is a physical point from which the beauty of the drawing/design/plan begins. But is there a non-physical point from where these plans emanate? Yes – in the mind.

Everything begins with a thought. You are reading this page because you thought to buy this book. Every action you perform, every meal eaten, every book read, every letter written, every song sung and every bank transaction you make, begins with a thought. The thought is the starting point of the action you perform. From that thought emanates an entire sequence of actions that stay in motion forever. Everything begins from a single thought, one of thousands upon thousands of thoughts you have in a day and more than one billion in a lifetime.

So what you're saying is that the dot or point within the circle represents a thought? Not exactly. Let's break it down further.
- Where does thought come from? What is thought?
- What gives us the ability for rational thought?
- How are we able to distinguish right from wrong?

Mary Baker Eddy (1821-1910), the founder of Christian Science, believed that thought and intelligence came from God as a single source, not from the brain. Eddy writes in her book *Science and Health with Key to the Scriptures:* 'To measure intellectual capacity by the size of the brain and strength by the exercise of muscle, is to subjugate intelligence, to make mind mortal, and to place this so-called mind at the mercy of material organisation and non-intelligent matter.' She goes on to say, 'Divine metaphysics, as revealed to spiritual understanding, shows clearly that all is Mind, and that Mind is God, omnipotence, omnipresence, omniscience – that is, all power, all presence, all science. Hence all is in reality the manifestation of Mind.'
- Is Baker correct?
- Is the source of our thoughts not our brain but rather God within us?
- Is the brain simply a reflexive organ responding to stimuli?

Ponder these questions and consider this: the brain is the most magnificent creation in the physical world. There is nothing in physical existence that compares with the majesty of the brain and its abilities. This three pound lump of grey and white matter, made up of about 75 percent water, consists of at least 60 percent fat, houses about 100,000 miles of blood vessels and consists of about 100 billion neurons, each of which has between 1,000 and 10,000 synapses. To call it a 'super machine' is an understatement. It's something the finest scientific minds cannot replicate, and perhaps never will. It is the true treasure beneath the hidden veil.

What powers the brain? Energy. But what sort of energy? We can't plug a dead brain into a power socket and get it working again. We can't put paddles on someone's head and yell 'clear!' and bring their brain back to life. What is the energy that powers the brain? Is it the soul?

Some believe the brain is the seat of the soul, and the pineal gland – the Third Eye located in the brain – is our attachment to the non-physical world. If the skull is the house of the brain, and the eyes are the window to the soul, then the two windows in this house let light into the brain and, in turn, into the soul.

Let's go even deeper. What is a soul? Is it only that which animates us or is it something more? You can't see a soul but can you feel it?

C. S. Lewis said, 'You don't have a soul, you *are* a soul. You have a body.'

Is he right? Are you eternal, endless, immortal energy existing at this moment in physical form? If you are eternal, endless, immortal energy, capable of animating flesh and bone, and giving that animation the ability to think rationally, to feel and act, are you god-like? Is the soul the part of you given spark by that which is your direct connection to God, the universe, the creator, the source, the divine intelligence?

This spark is best represented with a dot, which sits at the centre of a circle, and therefore at the centre of your soul.

The dot is your point of origin.

It is the tip of the pencil that first touched the canvas your life. It is the spark of creation from which you are forged – your divine spark – a piece of God, the universe, the source, the divine intelligence. There is no other starting point in your existence. From this point, you emanate as a soul and then as a physical being. This point remains a part of you forever. When your physical existence comes to an end, that is, when your body dies, the dot – the divine spark – remains. It is a flame never extinguished.

Let us move on to the circle that surrounds the point.

A circle has no beginning and no end and as such is a symbol of both immortality and deity. As ancient religions venerated the sun as a symbol of deity – all powerful, all seeing, above all, giving and sustaining life on the planet – the drawing of the sun as a circle became a representation of God. Indeed the astronomical symbol of the sun is, to this day, a point placed in the centre of a circle.

In having no beginning and no end, a circle represents immortality. What part of you is immortal? It is certainly not the flesh of your body. The immortal part of you is your soul. The soul is energy, and energy has no end. Energy from a power socket cannot die, it is only transformed. The same goes for the energy that powers your body and mind. The never-ending and eternal soul is represented by the circle. At the centre of that soul is a point, which is your divine spark.

Let's move onto the two perpendicular parallel lines on either side of the circle. Masonic ritual tells us that these two lines represent St John the Baptist and St John the Evangelist.

What do those two saints have to do with anything?

A fair question! Sadly, the newly made Entered Apprentice Freemason isn't told any more about why the two lines represent these two saints. And given that most

Masonic symbolism predates Christianity, it's kind of weird that we get two Christian saints as the explanation for a symbol older than the Common Era. That the feast days of the two saints correspond to the summer and winter solstices – June 21 and December 21 – offers a solar symbology for the two perpendicular lines.

The sun, moon and all the planets of the solar system function in harmony across expansive distances and affect life on Earth. Think about that for a moment. What a universe we live in! The sun, the moon and the planets all follow nature's strict rules about how they should move and perform. Each is a cog in an enormous wheel. Without one of these cogs, the wheel is incomplete and unable to perform its designated function.

As a microcosm of the universe, you also function according to a set of strict rules. If you operate in harmony and maintain balance, your body and soul achieves its purpose. If parts of you are out of whack, if your planets are out of orbit and do not obey the rules of nature, you will function improperly without balance or harmony.

The two perpendicular lines on either side of the circle represent Nature's Law (also known as Universal Law). In the Point within a Circle, the circle touches on both of these lines because, no matter what state of existence you achieve, you *must* operate within Nature's Law. If you stay within the bounds of Universal Law you cannot materially err, and you will achieve balance and harmony. Likewise, the sun operates within the law set down by the motion of the universe, that is, the sun operates between the solstices (the two parallel lines).

Personal choice is one of the great gifts of being human. Who or what gave us this gift? God, the universe, the creator, the source or whatever name you wish to use. Personal choice is given to us in the hope that the choices we make adhere to Universal Law, which is the glue that holds life together. If the Universal Law comes unstuck, chaos prevails.

Duality is part of Universal Law. Every cause has its effect; every effect has its cause; everything happens according to law; chance is but a name for law not recognised; there are many planes of causation, but nothing escapes the law no matter the plane of causation.

Buddha, Isaac Newton and Aristotle all spoke about duality. When you understand duality – cause and effect – you are able to take charge of your actions and understand the Golden Rule: don't do anything to someone else you wouldn't want done to you. It's that simple!

Good and bad, dark and light, loud and soft, up and down, in and out, happy or sad, callous or merciful – these are the dualities of life and the choices you make. These are the two perpendicular lines you must stay balanced between. The left perpendicular line polarises you; the right perpendicular line polarises you. Try to stay between the two lines, being not polarised by one or the other, whereby you experience the truest state of being, grace and harmony – the true you.

Place two horizontal lines above and below the circle. Now connect them to the two perpendicular lines. The result is a square surrounding the circle with the point at the centre. The square symbolises physical man. Man is nature and we experience nature in fours:

Four cardinal points: North, South, East, West
Four elements: Earth, Air, Water, Fire
Four states of matter: Solid, Liquid, Gas, Plasma
Four seasons: Summer, autumn (fall), winter, spring
Four limbs: two arms, two legs

To construct a square (man) requires the use of perpendicular lines (Universal Law). We are subject to laws ranging from the laws of our local municipality to those of our nation, international laws and, above all, Universal Law. Writes Laurence Dermott: 'Perfect legality is the only sure foundation for any society, and by it alone bodies of men are kept within their proper limits; for as soon as arbitrary power and physical force usurp the place of the laws of any society, it speedily becomes defunct.'[34]

Here then, in the seemingly simple symbol of a Point within a Circle between two parallel perpendicular lines, we have a blueprint of man. It is a representation of who we are and how we work. Let's break it down:

From our divine spark (the point), which is our connection to a higher power emanates our soul (the circle) which is immortal, divine energy. Every part of the circle (soul) is equidistant to the point (divine spark) giving balance.

The soul (circle) undertakes a physical experience when it inhabits a human body (the square). The body (square) is built around the already existing soul (circle) with a divine spark (point) at its centre.

In its human experience, the soul is subject to the material lusts and desires of the body. These lusts and desires are regulated through obedience to Universal Law (the two perpendicular lines) and achieving a balance of dualities, that is, achieving a state of non-polarisation with balance between the conscious and subconscious minds, the male and female aspects of your nature. If a person stays within these perpendicular lines, he cannot possibly err. The basis of Universal Law is the Golden Rule: do unto others as you would have them do to you. There is no greater lesson on how to live your life, and no greater law to govern life than the Golden Rule – and it is all contained in the Point within a Circle.

Freemasonry adds to this ancient symbol with the placement of the Holy Bible above the circle. If you're a Buddhist, a Hindu, a Muslim or a member of any other religion that doesn't recognise the Bible as its holy book, don't be dismayed. In Freemasonry, the Bible is known as the Volume of the Sacred Law and refers to the book of any religious system, from the Book of Mormon to the Qur'an, both of which I have seen open on Masonic altars. The Holy Bible above the Point within a Circle advises one to turn to the book of his faith for guidance (but feel free to examine the books of other faiths too!) Known as one of the Three Great Lights in Masonry (the other two being the square and compasses) Masons are taught to let the Volume of the Sacred Law be the 'rule and guide of their faith and practice'.

The Bible may seem like a lot of mumbo jumbo (especially all the Old Testament begetting) but it has stood the test of time on account of the important lessons it teaches. Whether you believe the stories to be fact or fiction doesn't matter. What matters are the lessons taught.

Is the story of Abraham, Sarah and Hagar true? Probably not, because eighty-nine year old women don't give birth. However, the lesson of the story is a good one – anything is possible!

Did Jacob really wrestle God all night through until morning, and then have his thigh bone popped out? Unlikely, but the lesson is one of detachment from carnal desires and the awakening of your Third Eye.

Did God really make a man, Adam, and a woman, Eve in a garden? Maybe he did. Or perhaps the Book of Genesis (note the word 'gene' in Genesis) tells the story of an atom (Adam) from which is taken an electron (Adam's rib), by which Adam turns into a positive atom. The electron is then placed in another atom, creating a negative ion (Eve). In this way God creates man in His own image – male and female (yin and yang / positive and negative).

Did Jonah really spend three days in the belly of a giant sea creature then get spewed up onto a beach? Probably not, but the story behind the story, which is a lesson in repentance, mercy and trust in a higher power, is important. These lessons have withstood the test of time because they were allegorised in an unforgettable, supernatural, action-packed tale.

Freemasonry has long recognised the Bible and other religious books as encrypted guidebooks to the great mysteries of the ages. The greatest of these mysteries is the reconnection of the soul to the source, which is the divine spark at your centre, the point within your circle.

Life Application
You are more than flesh and bone. Make a conscious effort daily to bring your circle

out of your square, that is, to exercise the aspects of your higher nature just as you would exercise the aspects of your physical (square) body.

At the end of each day ask yourself: Did I do unto someone else as I would have them do unto me? If the answer is 'No' examine your thought process and your actions, and determine how to prevent performing such actions tomorrow. In doing so, you learn how to follow Universal Law and live in balance between the perpendicular lines of your daily life.

The Point within a Circle is a symbol of your composition. You are a spiritual being inside a physical body with a divine spark at your centre.

The point represents the starting point of your creation. This is not your physical creation, which happened at the time of conception, but the creation of your true self, your soul.

A design, shape or plan begins with a single point. Take, for example, the drawing of a house. To begin drawing a house one must put pencil to paper, thus creating a point. However, even before the creation of this physical point, the hand receives the command from the brain. The brain receives information from the creative source of thought. This, then, is the very beginning; a conscious spark of creation from which emanates the entire process of drawing a house on a piece of paper.

The point (within the circle) is this conscious spark of creation from which you began. It sits in the centre of a circle, which is a shape with no beginning and no end. As such, a circle is a symbol of immortality. The soul, being pure energy, is immortal. Your soul cannot cease to exist. The circle represents your soul with a divine spark (the point) at its centre.

The perpendicular lines on either side of the circle form a square, symbolic of the physical self. The physical self exists within the boundaries of the perpendicular lines, representing Universal Law.

The symbolism of the Point within a Circle, therefore, is a picture of exactly who you are and how you need live for optimum performance. You are an eternal soul with a divine spark at your centre, residing in a physical body, which must operate within the rules of Universal Law to live in balance and harmony.

Ask Yourself
- Who do I want to be?
- How do I want the world to be different because I lived in it?
- What feeds my spirit?
- What makes my mouth drop in awe?
- Is my divine spark shining brightly or residing in the dim interior?
- What actions can I perform to make my divine spark radiate at my centre?

- If success is the unintended side effect of one's personal dedication to a cause greater than oneself, what am I in service of?
- What polarises me?
- How can I centre myself and become depolarised from that which polarises me?

The bouncer at the door of your mind
The Tyler

The positive thinker sees the invisible, feels the intangible, and achieves the impossible.

— Anonymous

Standing at the entry of every Masonic lodge is the Tyler. He carries a real sword or the symbol of a sword, usually in the form of a small jewel hung around his neck.

I visited a lodge where the Tyler twirled two swords in hand and another where he wielded a 50-inch medieval bastard sword. At a lodge I visited in Louisville, Kentucky, the Tyler wielded a tiny plastic cocktail sword, the kind used to skewer olives in a martini.

The use of the Tyler's sword dates back to the medieval operative craft guilds that closely guarded their trade secrets, and posted a sentry outside meeting places to protect against intrusion from the uninitiated. The sentry was known as an 'outer guard', 'guarder' or 'doorkeeper', and was often a junior apprentice without the qualifications to attend trade discussions.

When the operative guilds became speculative, the Tyler undertook the role of the outer guard. The word Tyler comes from old English and means the doorkeeper of an inn. In the early days of English Masonry, lodges met in taverns and inns, and employed the services of a Tyler to guard the doors of these establishments from unqualified, malicious, or curious people.

As one who traditionally laid tiles on a roof, the Masonic Tyler sat on the roof of the lodge to prevent prying eyes catching a sneak peek through openings in the tiles. Sometimes the weight proved too much for the eaves and the curious onlooker would fall through the roof, hence the word 'eavesdropper'.

In Freemasonry, it is the Tyler's duty to guard the entry of the lodge against anyone who is not a Mason (a cowan, in Masonic terms).

Is the Tyler allowed to physically use a sword to fight off potential gate-crashers?

Years before I became a Mason, a Masonic acquaintance of mine told me that, in fact, the Tyler was permitted to use his sword on anyone trying to enter a Masonic lodge without permission. 'He can stab someone with the sword and there's nothing the police can do about it because he is legally allowed to use that sword as a weapon.'

This acquaintance is the person I like to call a 'Postcard Mason'. He's the guy who wears the cufflinks, ring and lapel pin a week after being made an Entered Apprentice. He's the guy who when asked, 'What is Freemasonry and what do you do?' gives a smug smile and answers, 'I can't tell you, it's a secret. If I told you I'd have to kill you.' He's the guy who thinks the Tyler is legally entitled to use his sword to chop unwanted visitors in half. Yep, the Postcard Mason – he looks the part but lacks any understanding of the true lessons of Freemasonry.

There is a deep symbolism to the Tyler and his sword, which is referred to as the 'jewel of his office.'

A lodge cannot be opened for work and instruction unless properly tyled. The tyling process is known as the first great care of Masons and is a complete ritual of its own performed through a series of door knocks between the Tyler outside and an officer inside the lodge room. The duty of the Tyler is to keep tabs on those entering and exiting the lodge room, especially non-Masons who desire admission. Only those who are proven Masons and properly clothed – known in Masonic terms as being 'duly qualified' – are permitted entry to the lodge room. No person will ever enter a lodge room during a meeting without the Tyler first gaining approval from the Master of the lodge.

You may well be asking yourself, *why don't they just put a lock on the door? Wouldn't that serve the same purpose?* The simple answer is yes, but like most things Masonic, the Tyler is both operative and symbolic, and has a deeper meaning than merely acting as a guard.

To understand the symbolism of the Tyler, think of him as both a bouncer on the door of an exclusive club and as a key part of the representation of yourself. The Masonic lodge being a symbol of your mind, body and soul, the Tyler is symbolic of a guard protecting the entrance to your inner self.

Tyling a lodge is the first great care of Masons, which offers indication as to the importance of the process. Using the lodge as a representation of yourself, the symbolism of the Tyler tells you that it is of the utmost importance to tyle yourself every day, allowing you to function optimally as an upstanding and productive member of society.

If you are the lodge and the lodge is you, it is imperative that you guard your mind from the entry of anything unworthy of admittance. This doesn't mean to physically hold a sword and fend off people unworthy of being in your life, but rather to guard your thoughts against negativity. You must tyle your mind and keep your thoughts pure and positive, permitting entry only to those thoughts of positive influence. Your personal Tyler ensures that your thoughts are pure and unpolluted.

Your inner Tyler is focused, sharp, and always on the ball. He knows you're capable of impure thoughts and it's his job to make sure such thoughts are blocked from entering your mind. Your Tyler allows entry only to those thoughts that are helpful and useful for personal growth, for the betterment of yourself, and the improvement of your environment. As your Tyler is part of you, remember that you alone have the power to admit or dismiss any thought.

Tyling yourself is all about positive thinking. It's as simple as that!

The Tyler's sword is a symbol that teaches you to prevent the approach of every unworthy thought. Here then is the true duty of the Tyler: he is at the entrance of your mind, guarding it like a bouncer against thoughts that do not have permission to enter. By blocking negativity from entering your mind, you safeguard your physical and psychical self.

Negative thoughts damage both the physical body and the spirit, just as a drunk or unruly patron damages a nightclub. This is not some form of New Age thinking but a fact upon which traditional systems, such as Chinese medicine, base their practices. Acupuncture is a medical practice originating in ancient China, perhaps even as early as the Stone Age. Hieroglyphic discoveries dating from the Shang Dynasty (1600-1100 BCE) suggest the performance of acupuncture at that time.[35] The focus of acupuncture is to remedy the body's energy flow by applying pressure to energy paths known as meridian points. Negative thoughts and emotions, such as fear, sadness and anger, directly impact these meridian points and have a detrimental effect on the body's major organs.

The mind and body are connected. One affects the other. As above (the mind) so below (the body) Negative thoughts impact the physical body and may cause sickness. You can, literally, think yourself sick. A study published in the American Journal of Cardiology claims that people with a high level of stress have a 27 percent higher risk of developing coronary heart disease.[36]

Superstitions, which are thought processes, may also serve to deteriorate the body. Why is this? Not because a superstition is proven to physically exist (ie: thinking someone has placed a hex on you) but because the person who believes in superstition impacts their health through negative beliefs.

In the medical community, such manifestation is known as medical student disease. Medical students commonly develop symptoms of the illness they are studying. As the mind becomes paranoid of the illness, the body physically manifests this paranoia.

Negative thoughts feed the amygdala, which is a mass of nuclei located in the temporal lobes of the brain near the hippocampus. Stimulation of the amygdala causes intense emotion, such as aggression or fear. The amygdala reacts to negative thoughts in various ways, including the activation of your sympathetic nervous system. This process is almost incomprehensibly quick. While it takes you around 300 milliseconds to become aware of a disturbing thought, the amygdala reacts to such thoughts in around 20 milliseconds!

A negative thought acts as a red flag to the amygdala, which sends out an alert that activates the brain's stress response, otherwise known as fight-or-flight response. The amygdala receives perceptual information related to external threats, i.e. thinking yourself sick. When the amygdala interprets something as a danger, it sends signals to the brain's command centre, the hypothalamus. When the nervous system operates in fight-or-flight mode, the body's self-repair mechanisms function improperly and the body becomes exposed to illness.

As above, so below: if you think yourself sick, you risk making yourself sick. If you think yourself cursed, you risk the body manifesting such.

Reality originates in the mental. Therefore, you have no greater goal as a human being than self-mastery, which, in essence, is mastery over your words and thoughts, which in turn leads to the illumination of your divine spark. If your thoughts become your reality – your thoughts become your words and actions – then mastery over these thoughts is imperative. There is no greater power governing your life than your thoughts. What you think manifests in your physical reality. Through your thoughts, you attract and resist. Awareness of every thought, therefore, is of the greatest importance. How you shape your mind and use your mental energy – where you place the Tyler upon the boundaries of your thinking to determine your thought patterns – creates your existence.

As tyling the lodge is the first great care of Masons when convened, tyling your mind should be your first care before attempting any further advancement in personal betterment. The problem is, of course, that in the beginning of any work on ourselves the greatest hurdle we experience is our innate disquiet of mind.

How many times have you failed to fall asleep when your body is tired because your mind just won't quit? Your eyes and muscles are heavy but your mind is in its own world, happily thinking this and that while your tired body begs for it to shut up.

The mind, by its very nature, is erratic and unconstrained. To achieve self-improvement and become aware of your inner self requires a hushed and focused mind, free from negative emotions and the distractions of material things.

To reach the state of consciousness and awareness to attain this clarity of mind, you need willpower and the ability to direct the mind toward your end aim, which is the illumination of your divine spark, your centre, your higher self. You need to safeguard your mind against preoccupation with material possessions, ego, lusts and desires, and stop the mental processes that cause disharmony. What you need is a strong, forceful and vigilant bouncer standing behind the velvet rope at the doorway of your mind.

The Tyler in a Masonic lodge also has the duty of making sure that the candidate for Freemasonry is properly prepared. Symbolically this pertains to making sure that the people we interact with on a daily basis are good and positive influences on our lives. Admitting people into your life is at your complete discretion. You must employ your personal Tyler, your life's own bouncer, to ensure that only positive people gain entry to your life. Your personal Tyler – symbolic of your conscience, common sense, judgment and the safeguard of your morals and standards – must prevent you from entering into contact (admitting to your own lodge) negative people who harbour hatred, lust and ill intent.

The symbolic lesson of the Tyler's duty should be applied to all aspects of life. Make it your first great care to see that you are properly guarded against bad thoughts. When you awaken in the morning, make a conscious effort to tyle your mind and invite only positive thoughts into your personal lodge. Remember, the amygdala responds quickly to negative thoughts. The reaction of the amygdala provides a knee-jerk response that may cause you to overreact to the world around you. Such reactions in the morning may subconsciously trouble you the entire day. An awareness of the amygdala's mechanism through tyling your mind enables you to effectively still the ill effects of negative thinking and recover your peace of mind.

As you go through your day and interact with others in personal and professional dealings, make a concerted effort to constantly tyle your mind, admitting only positive and productive thoughts.

The process of changing the way you think from negative to positive begins with changing your mindset. This change of mindset is applied by redirecting the flow of negativity into a flow of positivity through your reaction to daily events. You can't always control the events that impact your life but you can control your reactions to such events. You must realise that you cannot change the past and it is a waste of precious energy to obsess over the future. One is written into the annals of time and gone forever, that is, it can never be relived; the other will never come as you can only live in the present.

Negative thoughts enter your mind more often than not because you are preoccupied with the past or the future – both of which you cannot change in the present, which is the only place in which you exist. You can affect your future through your present actions but you cannot live and enact the future, only the present. Ultimately, the future and the past exist completely as mental projections. They have no reality beyond the way in which your mind contemplates them and plays them over and over again. By attuning your mind to the present, you will eliminate the guilt and resentment of the past and the worry of the future, both of which cannot be altered in the present.

Take the scenario of oversleeping, even with an alarm clock. You sleep fifteen minutes past your alarm and wake up in a panic, worried that you will miss your 9am meeting. You wash your face, brush your teeth, and get dressed in a hurry, all the while stressed and anxious (this is the amygdala processing thoughts of being late).

You rush out the door; get in your car and drive recklessly, weaving in and out of traffic, posing a threat to yourself and others as you desperately try to make it to your meeting on time. Your mind projects images of what you think will be: an angry boss and annoyed co-workers. You push down on the gas a little more. Your mind projects even further. Suddenly you imagine getting fired. You're out of a job. You're scouring newspapers and online sites for work. You're lining up for a welfare cheque. Your life is spiralling out of control.

Do you stop to realise that this is only a projection of your mind, and that your life is not really out of control? Of course not! You continue to drive dangerously. Your pulse races. Your mouth dries. You sweat uncontrollably. You yell and curse. Your world is falling apart – in your mind.

Do you stop to think about the present, the only time you can affect, and how you can alter your situation by reacting to the present?

Do you consider it better to arrive safely at your destination than to get into a wreck?

Do you consider making a call and calmly telling your colleagues that you're running late and to start the meeting without you?

Do you tell them not to worry if you're a few minutes late as you are completely prepared and have all the information they require for the meeting?

Do you consider relaying some of that information now, in the present, which they can use at the start of the meeting until your arrival?

Are you using your inner Tyler to deny the entrance of negativity into your mind and focus on the present, on the positives, and set thoughts of the present into a productive course of action?

To worry about the past and obsess over the future is fruitless. Both are out of your control. Centre your focus on the present and concentrate on walking justly and uprightly in whatever it is you are doing in the moment.

Think of yourself as being in the middle of a minefield. You can see the end of the minefield, and you can't turn back to where you entered or you will never reach your destination. You must go forward but you can only do so one baby step at a time. Each baby step is the now. It is the most important and the only action in your life at this very moment. Take that step truly, safely and with faith that you will reach your destination. Now take the next step, and the next, and the next, one at a time. Eventually you will reach your destination, only to see that there is another horizon before you.

There is always another horizon, just as there is always a trail left behind. Your aim is to reach the horizon but you can only do so through your actions in the present. Rush forward and you will get blown to pieces. Backtrack and your goal becomes more distant. Concentrate on the current step, on maintaining balance, remaining upright and navigating the minefield successfully. To do so requires concentration and positivity, as does your journey through an upright and well balanced life, one small step at a time.

There is a method you can use to tyle your mind. It's a simple visualisation technique I developed and has proven effective for me in tyling myself.

Imagine a Tyler. Most of the Tylers I have met are elderly gentlemen with bushy eyebrows, wrinkled foreheads and wise old eyes. You can visualise a Tyler of any appearance you so desire, but for me he is an old, friendly but no-nonsense gentleman wearing a dinner suit and holding a medieval long sword, the tip of which rests on the ground between his feet.

My Tyler stands in front of a wooden door on which is a large brass knocker. The door is the entrance to my mind. Any thought wishing to enter my mind must go through this door, which means first getting past my Tyler.

When a bad thought pops into my head, I envision the Tyler blocking its passage. The bad thought may be persistent but my Tyler stands steadfast. When the thought eventually disappears, my Tyler grips the brass knocker and delivers three loud knocks to signify that the would-be intruder (the bad thought) is gone.

I have also used this method of visualisation to successfully get rid of headaches. To do this, I visualise the door to my Lodge opened, as the headache is already in my head. I then visualise the door closing and the Tyler knocking loudly three times to signify that the headache has left my head. I do not prescribe this as a surefire remedy for curing headaches but this visualisation technique has worked for me on many occasions.

If you're more fantasy-oriented, another good visualisation technique is to generate a mental picture of Gandalf the wizard from *Lord of the Rings*. Picture Gandalf with a staff in one hand and a sword in the other; facing off against the Balrog that dwelt in the depths of Moria that he faced on the Bridge of Khazad-dum. The Balrog represents a negative thought attempting to enter your mind. As the Balrog sought to consume Gandalf in fire, the wizard stood firm and told the creature: 'You cannot pass'.[37] In doing so, Gandalf defeats the Balrog, just as you can defeat the flame of negativity that seeks to consume you.

As you go through your daily activities, keep in mind the words of the Greek philosopher, Epictetus (55-135 CE):

> 'Nothing truly stops you. Nothing truly holds you back. For your own will is always within your control. Sickness may challenge your body. But are you merely your body? Lameness may impede your legs. But you are not merely your legs. Your will is bigger than your legs. Your will needn't be affected by an incident unless you let it.'

Life Application

Life is a constant flow of thoughts. Your thoughts can be quietened but they can't be stopped. They're with you from the moment you're born to the moment you die and, most likely, beyond death too.

Left unchecked, your thoughts may run free, unbridled, and adversely affect your life. However, you have the power to tame the beast, still the voices in your head and grant entry to those thoughts you deem worthy of admittance.

Your inner Tyler stands at the doorway to your mind, and your mind is the doorway to your body. Protect your mind and in turn protect your body from negative thoughts by tyling yourself on a constant basis.

You are the guardian of your thoughts, your mind's bouncer. Eckart Tolle wrote: 'The primary cause of unhappiness is never the situation but your thoughts about it.'[38]

Be aware of negative thoughts and the detrimental effects they have on your physical and mental wellbeing. Actively work to block and remove from your life negative thoughts and negative people. Take baby steps to ensure that your thoughts and actions are positive, uplifting, and serve the purpose of elevating you above your material/crude/animal nature.

To achieve elevation you must focus on the present. The present is all there is and all you have in the physical world. The concept of time may change on other planes of existence but you do not function on these planes – at least not yet. All you have is now. Accept it and work to improve the present. The past cannot be relived and the future never comes. What was yesterday's future is the present, and the present is tomorrow's past.

When you focus on now, you realise that there is a confined space for your personal bouncer to keep safe. Narrow your focus on what is within your control – the present moment – and make it secure, positive and fruitful.

As Buddha said: 'the secret of health for both mind and body is not to mourn for the past, worry about the future, or anticipate troubles, but to live in the present moment wisely and earnestly.'

Be vigilant guarding the doorway to your thoughts. Use your personal Tyler to block negativity, and allow only positive energy to feed and fuel your mind.

Ask Yourself
- What was the first thought I had upon waking?
- What was the first negative thought to enter my mind today?
- Am I still thinking about that negative thought?
- Why am I letting this negative thought exist in my mind when I have the ability to block it out?
- Are there people or situations in my life that cause me anxiety and pain?
- Picture a situation that causes you anxiety and ask: Can I use my Tyler to close the door to my personal lodge, give three loud knocks and eject this anxiety from my mind?
- If my physical reality is created from my thoughts, what do I want to manifest in my life?

All a buzz
The beehive

If the bee disappeared off the surface of the globe, then man would only have four years of life left.

— Albert Einstein

The third degree of Freemasonry, known as the Sublime Degree of Master Mason, features more symbols than the previous two degrees combined. In addition to the three symbolic working tools of the degree – the pencil, compasses and skirrett (the trowel in American Freemasonry) – the newly raised Master Mason is presented a series of 'emblems', one of which is the beehive.

At face value, the symbolism of the beehive seems straightforward: it represents industry and many working together as one. However, like the complex creatures that inhabit its honeycomb interior, there is nothing simple about the beehive and its allegory.

Freemasonry teaches that the beehive is an emblem of industry, and recommends the practice of industriousness. We are all created as rational and intelligent beings, and as such should ever be industrious. Freemasonry teaches that a man should never remain stagnant nor lazy while others around him are in need, especially when it is in his power to relieve them without damage to himself.

A simple explanation of the beehive's symbolism, right?

The beehive is a visual call to arms to work harder and help out one another, which makes sense as the bee is probably the hardest working and most altruistic creature in existence. A bee will fly around 800 km (500 miles) in a lifetime, hauling loads half its body weight. Bees work so hard that they drop dead from exhaustion three weeks after their maiden flight! And all of this hard work is done not for individual gain but for the greater good of the hive.

Is it really that simple? Does the enduring emblem of the beehive in the third and highest degree of Freemasonry teach us only to work hard and to do so together? Sheesh, my dad taught me the same lesson when I landed my first paper route!

Like all Masonic symbols, we need to delve deeper into the honey pot to discover the true reward of knowledge.

Greek mythology tells us that Zeus sent out two eagles flying around the Earth. Where the two birds met was deemed to be the centre of the world or the 'navel' of the Earth. The birds are said to have met at Delphi, a city on the slopes of Mount Parnassus, overlooking the Gulf of Corinth, a hundred miles north of Athens. An Omphalos stone was placed to mark the centre of the Earth and would later become the inner sanctum of the shrine of the Delphic oracle, in the Temple of Apollo. The Pythia, chief priestess of the Temple of Apollo, was anointed with the title 'the Delphic Bee.' She was considered the Queen Bee of Ancient Greece and her rituals required honey to induce states of spiritual rapture.

Omphalos is defined as: *1. the navel; umbilicus; 2. the central point.* These definitions are apt for a stone placed in what would be considered the navel (central point) of the world. Intriguingly, the Omphalos at Delphi was shaped to resemble a beehive.

As you can see, the Greeks revered bees. They believed honey was the food of the divinities. Zeus, the King of the Gods, was born in a cave and raised by bees, who fed him a diet of milk and honey.[39] The Ancient Greeks also held the belief that bees were connected to the human soul. Philosopher and mathematician Porphyry of Tyre (234-305 CE), author of *Philosophy from Oracles* which discussed, among other subjects, the nature of astrological fate[40], believed that bees carried human souls to earth. These souls, held within the bees, were enticed into an early existence by the allure of material delectations such as honey. Indeed, the cave in which Zeus was raised still exists in Crete and is named 'Cave of the Bee'. To this day, Greeks use the cave for their Easter rituals – a celebration of resurrection and of the soul.

Ancient Greek philosopher Plato (428-348 BCE), and playwright Sophocles (496-406 BCE), attributed their oratory skills to the belief that, as small children, bees landed on their mouths.

The Greeks weren't the only ancient culture to revere the honey bee. The Ancient Egyptians developed methods of advanced apiculture as far back as 3000 BCE. Menes, the first King of Egypt, who ruled somewhere between 5000 BCE to 4000 BCE, was called 'The Beekeeper', a title bestowed on all subsequent Pharaohs.[41]

Depictions of bees and honey are prevalent on many Egyptian carvings including the Flamic and Pamphilic obelisks, the obelisk of Luxor, the pillars of the Temple of Karnak and on statues of Rameses II.[42] The Rosetta Stone, which dates to 196 BCE, is etched with pictures of bees. Royal tombs in Egypt also show the importance of beekeeping and honey, including the enormous sarcophagus of Rameses II, which includes numerous pictures of honey bees. Foodstuffs created by bees, such as pots of honey, honeycombs and honey cakes, were placed near the sarcophagi as food for the gods. Even Alexander the Great requested that his body be wrapped in honey upon his death.

References to bees are found in Hindu texts as far back as 1500 BCE. To this day, Buddhists donate honey to monks during the festival of Madhu Purnima, translated as 'honey full-moon'. The day commemorates Buddha's retreat into the Parileyya forest where he was fed fruit by an elephant and honeycomb by a monkey.

Buddha wasn't the only great teacher to eat honey. In the New Testament, the Book of Luke tells us that honey was the first food eaten by Christ after his resurrection: 'Jesus said, Have you got anything to eat? And they offered him a piece of broiled fish and a honeycomb, which he ate.'

For thousands of years, in numerous cultures, the bee has been associated with esoteric and spiritual endeavours, and aptly so. There is, perhaps, no more altruistic creature in existence than the honey bee, as summarised in a statement of St John Chrysostom (349-407 CE) in his twelfth homily: 'The bee is more honoured than other animals, not because she labours, but because she labours for others. Indeed, the bee works unceasingly for the common good of the hive, and obeys without question what sometimes appears to be an inequitable hierarchy.'

I get it, you may be thinking. *Bees work hard for one another, so we too should work hard not just for ourselves but for each other.*

There's still more symbology to the beehive than meets the eye. Let's delve deeper.

Hiroto Fujiyoshi, a Japanese beekeeper, writes of the construction of the beehive: 'The honey bee is an architect surpassed only by man. The structure of a honeycomb is the perfection of symmetry, precision, arrangement and strength. We cannot know what bees are really thinking, but it is safe to say that they are trying to create the maximum amount of space with a minimal amount of material. The hexagon is said to be the most efficient in this regard because the circle or octagon create gaps and the triangle or square makes the area smaller.'[43] It is no coincidence that the hexagon features in Masonic symbolism as the inner shape revealed when laying a downward-pointing triangle (as above; universe into matter) over an upright-pointing triangle (so below; matter into higher learning). This symbol, known as the hexagram, six pointed star or Seal of Solomon, represents balance and the harmonisation of spirit and matter. Fittingly, there is no creature in existence that lives in a more harmonious society than the honey bee.

The beehive, therefore, is seen as a perfectly constructed environment inside of which its inhabitants work and reside in peace. As such it is a symbol of utopian existence crafted by harmony.

Harmony is one of the supports of the Masonic lodge, which as you have learned is emblematic of a human being. For someone to achieve a utopian state in their own existence, every aspect of their being – body, mind, soul (material, mental and spiritual) – must be in harmony. Just as the hexagon construction of the honeycomb leaves no spaces between its cells so must each of us leave no gaps in our own physical, mental, and spiritual construction. All must fit together in perfect harmony to allow for the greatest productivity – the bee, as stated above, being arguably the most productive creature in all creation.

A honey bee's sting proves fatal not for the recipient of the sting, but for the bee itself. The honey bee's stinger is made of two barbed lancets. Once the sting goes into its target it cannot be retrieved. The stinger is left behind along with muscles, nerves and part of the bee's digestive tract, resulting in an abdominal rupture that kills the bee.[44]

The death of a bee after causing pain to another creature is symbolic of an action opposing the Universal Law. As discussed in earlier chapters, the Universal Law states all beings are sovereign and have free will to express their creative urges in any way they choose, but no being has the right to violate and harm others. All beings, guided by the Universal Law, are prohibited from performing actions that would harm another. We should all respect the rights and boundaries of others.

The symbolic lesson of a bee sting is simple: do unto others as you would have them do unto you. Writes George H. Steinmatz, in *Freemasonry: Its Hidden Meaning*: 'The bee obeys the law, therefore "peace and harmony prevail" within the hive. When man as unerringly conforms to that same Universal Law, he will find that "peace and harmony prevail" in his life.'[45]

To realise the most important symbolic teaching of the beehive, let's go back to the Omphalos, that beehive shaped stone in the Temple of Apollo at Delphi, said to be located at the navel (centre) of the world.

The top of the Omphalos is curved in shape as the top of a beehive. This curvature resembles the symbolic keystone of the Mark Master and Royal Arch degrees of York Rite Masonry. In the ritual of the Mark Master degree, the keystone previously discarded by the builders is recovered from the rubbish and used to complete the building of the temple. In operative masonry, a keystone is a stone that holds together an arch. An amazing feat of early engineering, the curved keystone allows builders to incorporate components such as windows and doorways into a building without sacrificing the structure's strength. The fitting of the keystone allows for more natural light to enter into a structure.

As a symbol of completion, the message taught by the keystone – the top of the Omphalos, the beehive, the final piece of the puzzle – is obvious.

The keystone (heightened knowledge of material, physical and spiritual learning; mind, body and soul; mastery over every aspect of oneself) which was previously discarded by the builders (knowledge discarded in favour of material desires) is recovered from the rubbish (a material-centric existence) and used to complete the building (our own education) of the temple (ourselves).

Light in Freemasonry is symbolic of knowledge (illumination, enlightenment). Thus the keystone completes the structure, allows light to enter (true knowledge or mastery over the material, and mental, to achieve the spiritual) and is the final piece in the completion of ourselves into beings of the highest state of existence.

'Knowledge is the most genuine and real of human treasures; for it is Light, as Ignorance is Darkness,' writes Albert Pike. 'It is the *development* of the human soul, and its acquisition the *growth* of the soul, which at the birth of man knows nothing, and therefore, in one sense, may be said to *be* nothing. It is the seed, which has in it the *power* to grow, to acquire, and by acquiring to be developed, as the seed is developed into the shoot, the plant, the tree.'[46]

Pike goes on to say that the pursuit of knowledge must be a selfless task, further reinforcing the symbolism of the beehive, the bee being the most altruistic creature in all creation:

'To learn, to attain knowledge, to be wise, is a necessity for every truly noble soul; to teach, to communicate that knowledge, to share that wisdom with others and not churlishly to lock up his exchequer, and place a sentinel at the door to drive away the needy, is equally an impulse of a noble nature, and the worthiest work of man.'[47]

We each have a navel. It is better known as our belly button. This scar in the middle (centre) of the abdomen is where our umbilical cord was removed after birth. Our umbilical cord (also known as the navel cord) is what once connected us to our mother. It was the conduit between us as a growing embryo and the placenta of our mother, which fashioned us with oxygenated, nutrition-rich blood for our growth. When our umbilical cord was cut away, we were left to grow entirely on our own without physical attachment to our mother.

The Omphalos, as the beehive at the navel of the world, symbolises that you were once linked to a higher source which fed your soul. The removal of your umbilical cord symbolically detached you from this higher source – from the centre, the Omphalos, the beehive. Detached and alone, you must look for a way to return to this centre and be reunited with God, nature, the universe, a higher spirit or whatever name you wish to call it. When you achieve this reconnection to the centre, a place in which your body, mind and soul (material, mental and spiritual) is in complete harmony (the hexagonal honeycomb of a beehive) you will be rewarded with the sweetness of your greatest self (honey) – a perfect soul.

This lesson was taught in many ancient mystery schools. The Pythagoreans understood that the soul was harmony and that the great cosmic harmony with the soul – reconnection to the centre – is the true destiny of existence. Alcmaeon of Croton (5th century BCE), a medical writer and scientist-philosopher, was a pupil of the Pythagorean system. He wrote that the soul is immortal because it resembles immortal beings, in that it is always in motion. The same can be said of the beehive – like the soul, it is always in motion and working for altruistic purposes.

Writes C. C. Zain, in *Ancient Masonry: The Spiritual Meaning of Masonic Degrees, Rituals and Symbols:* 'As the bee exercises industry and prudence in gathering honey while it may, storing it for use during the long winter, so should man industriously gather experiences, and through a constructive attitude toward them store them properly to serve as spiritual nourishment when the summer of physical life is supplanted by the icy winter of death'.[48]

The amazing feats of bees are therefore symbolic of the amazing things we are all capable of when we learn how to reconnect with our centre, our Omphalos, our beehive. And if you still don't think the bee is a truly astonishing creature, consider these bee facts:

- An individual honey bee can fly as far as five miles from the hive in search of food.
- A honey bee colony will fly as far as 55,000 miles to make just one pound of honey. It requires about two million flowers being tapped by bees to make one pound of honey.[49]
- Honey is the only food which contains every nutrient that a human needs to survive, including water content.
- Once honey bee eggs hatch into worker larvae, they'll be fed around 1,300 times per day.
- Honey bees fly up to 15 mph and beat their wings 200 times per second or 12,000 beats per minute[50]
- The honey bee is the only insect that produces food eaten by man.
- Honey bees pack a million neurons into a brain that measures a mere cubic millimetre[51]

Life Application

Albert Einstein once said: 'If the bee disappeared off the surface of the globe, then man would only have four years of life left.' Crazy, right? Bees are a vital part of man's existence and symbolically bees and the beehive teach us several important life lessons.

Bees are amazing creatures in both their work ethic and organisation. They're committed to the task of a healthy hive and depend on one another for survival, recognising that though they are individuals they are also connected as one with the hive, just as you are connected as one with the universe.

The beehive is a symbol of utopian existence fashioned by harmony. Harmony is one of the supports of Freemasonry. Given that the Masonic lodge is a representation of the individual, for someone to achieve a utopian state they must achieve a harmonious fusing of the three aspects of their make up: body, mind, and soul.

Just as the hexagonal building blocks of a honeycomb leave no gap between its cells, so must each of us leave no gaps in our physical, mental, and spiritual aspects. All must fit together in perfect harmony to allow for the greatest productivity. This is the secret of the bees. Harmony leads to productivity.

The bee itself is symbolic of Universal Law. A honey bee's sting kills the bee. That the bee dies after causing pain to another creature is symbolic of an action opposing the Universal Law. It doesn't matter how much of a hard-working member of society you are, go against Universal Law and you will suffer the consequences.

Universal Law states that all beings are sovereign and have free will to express their creative urges in any way they choose, but no being has the right to violate and harm others. The bee chooses to express its creative urge in the production of honey, the lifeline of the entire hive. However, as good as this intention is for the individual, it does not place them 'above the law', so to speak, in relation to Universal Law. If a bee obeys the law, peace and harmony prevail. Similarly, if a man obeys Universal Law, peace and harmony prevail in his life. How can it not? After all, at the heart of Universal Law is the maxim: Do unto others as you would have them do unto you.

The lesson of the beehive continues with an explanation of the structure of the hive itself, the top of which is in the form of an arch.

In operative masonry, a keystone is a stone that holds together an arch. The fitting of the keystone allows for more natural light to enter into a structure. As such, the keystone symbolises heightened knowledge of material, physical and spiritual learning. It is mastery over every aspect of oneself. This knowledge is necessary to complete the structure which, in this case, is you.

You must allow the light of knowledge to illuminate your life.

The lesson of the beehive concludes with the Omphalos, or navel, which looks like a beehive. The navel is your physical centre, at which you were once connected to your source of survival, your mother, by an umbilical cord. The severing of the umbilical cord at birth represents detachment from this source. Symbolically this source, this mother, is God, nature, the universe, a higher spirit or whatever you wish to call it.

Through knowledge, you achieve a reconnection to this source at your centre, a place in which your body, mind, and soul (material, mental and spiritual) is in complete harmony. When these three aspects of yourself become one, you will be rewarded with the sweetness of honey, which is symbolic of your greatest self, a perfect soul.

Ask Yourself
- Do I feel a sense of disconnection from my higher / spiritual self?
- Are my actions altruistic like the honey bee or selfish?
- Did I perform a selfish act today and if I had not acted selfishly, how would the result of my action have differed?
- To what extent will I go to reconnect with my higher self?
- How can I become more of a team player, for the betterment of others as well as for myself?
- What is the sweetest reward I am receiving in my life at the moment? Is there a sweeter reward I aspire towards?
- Am I working as hard as I can to achieve my goals?
- Is there someone specific in my life I can help to achieve their goals?

The only way is up
The winding staircase

Never look backwards or you'll fall down the stairs.
— Rudyard Kipling

The second degree of Freemasonry, known as the Fellowcraft degree, contains one of the most discussed, debated, and rewarding of all symbols – a winding staircase.

Rich in symbolism, the winding staircase also has an operative history as part of King Solomon's Temple. Said to be the grandest building ever constructed, Solomon's Temple was located on Mount Zion in ancient Jerusalem before its destruction by Nebuchadnezzar II after the Siege of Jerusalem in 587 BCE.

Divinely inspired, the temple's ornate beauty and architectural design is said to have no match in history. This makes Solomon's Temple the perfect symbol for the human being – the greatest and most beautiful creation in nature. It is the duty of each of us to construct our own spiritual temple, 'that house not made with hands, eternal in the heavens.' (Corinthians 5:1) This duty is at the very core of Masonic teaching, and is best described by Albert Pike who wrote: 'Freemasonry is the subjugation of the Human that is in man by the Divine; the conquest of the appetites and passions by the moral sense and reason; a continual effort, struggle and warfare of the spiritual against the material and sensual.'[52]

The Bible details the winding

staircase of Solomon's Temple in 1 Kings, 6:1-8: 'The doorway for the lowest side chamber was on the right side of the house; and they would go up by winding stairs to the middle story, and from the middle to the third.'

Solomon's Temple comprised three main areas, each of which is allegorically and symbolically significant in Masonic teaching.

The Ground Floor

The Middle Chamber

The Sanctum Sanctorum

The most important of these areas, the Sanctum Sanctorum, also known as the Holy of Holies, was the resting place of the Ark of the Covenant containing the Ten Commandments given by God to Moses. As the presence of God was believed to reside in the Sanctum Sanctorum, only the High Priest entered the space, and then only once a year on the Day of Atonement.

Allegorically the three areas of the temple refer to the three-fold character of a person, being the body (ground floor), mind (middle chamber) and soul (sanctum sanctorum). It is the knowledge and perfection of these three components of human design that one should strive to achieve and which is only accomplished in this order. Control must be exerted over the material aspect of your nature (ground floor) before it can be exerted over the mental aspect (middle chamber). An advanced mental state must be achieved before development of the spirit (sanctum sanctorum).

The symbolism of the winding stairs is introduced in the Fellowcraft lecture, which explains that the workmen of the temple climbed a set of winding stairs to reach the middle chamber. There, after proving their identification through use of a grip and a password, they received their wages and were recorded as faithful workmen (take note of the word 'faithful' here). While these grips and passwords contain their own important symbolism, our focus here is on the winding design of the staircase.

You may be thinking, *Big deal! Maybe a winding staircase looked better in the temple than a straight staircase.*

Nothing in Freemasonry exists simply for the purpose of existing. Every symbol has its place and even a seemingly minute detail, such as a winding staircase as opposed to a straight staircase, is laden with important symbolism.

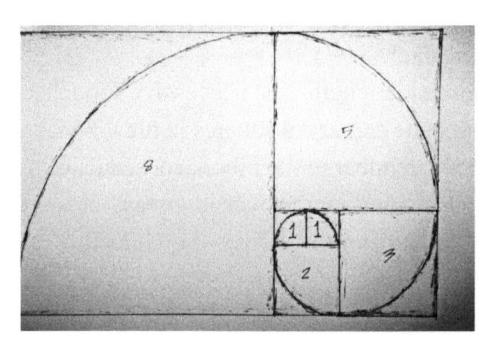

So why does the Masonic staircase wind?

Picture yourself driving up a mountain. To reach the top requires driving up a winding road. A straight road would be shorter but a car cannot reach a peak by way of a straight line. The only way to reach the top of a mountain is by a winding road.

Masonry is a progressive science and a system of education that teaches self-betterment. Education does not occur in an instant. True education takes time. The Entered Apprentice may be likened to a child who has just begun his education and is well on his way to becoming a Fellowcraft, where he reaches adulthood. As the Entered Apprentice progresses in his education from the allegorical ground floor of King Solomon's Temple to the middle chamber by way of a flight of winding stairs, his educational process takes on the form of a spiral, not a straight line.

Education is a spiral process. The staircase of the temple symbolises the progression of the individual's education in life, which takes a spiral shape.

In his 1960 book, *The Process of Education*, author Jerome Bruner, a psychologist who has made significant contributions to human cognitive psychology and cognitive learning theory in educational psychology,[53] discusses the idea of spiral curriculum. Spiral curriculum takes the approach that a child can learn any subject if it is broken into strands or ideas that are repeatedly taught to the child with an increasing degree of complexity year after year.

Let's make a further observation about spirality. If man is part of nature (which he is) and nature is spiral (which it is) then it serves to reason that man's educational process should be spiral in its makeup, not straight lined.

What do I mean by nature is spiral? I'm sure you've heard of something called the Fibonacci sequence.

The Fibonacci sequence, named after Leonardo of Pisa, better known as Fibonacci, is the numbers in the following integer sequence:[54]

$$0, 1, 1, 2, 3, 5, 8, 13, 21, 34, 55, 89, 144...$$

Introduced into Western mathematics through Fibonacci's 1202 book *Liber Abaci*,[55] the numbers in the Fibonacci sequence can be traced to usage in ancient times as far back as 450 BCE and the Indian author Pingala.[56]

If one draws a tiling with squares whose side lengths are successive Fibonacci numbers, then draws arcs connecting the opposite corners of squares in the Fibonacci tiling, a Fibonacci spiral is created. Divide any number in the Fibonacci sequence by the one before it, for example 21/13 or 34/21, and the answer is always close to 1.61803. This is known as the Golden Ratio and from it derives the Golden Mean Spiral (Golden Mean Geometry).

The Fibonacci sequence is referred to as Nature's numbering system. The Golden

Mean Spiral is prevalent through all nature and is seen in the close inspection of hurricanes, galaxies, seashells, snails, the flight patterns of birds and insects, the human ear, the leaf arrangement in plants, and human DNA. Fibonacci spiral patterns appear abundantly in plant life that forms in spirals such as rose petals, pineapples, pinecones, ferns and sunflowers. The spirals created by the Fibonacci sequence curve around a surface both clockwise and counterclockwise, otherwise known as sinister form and dexter form.

The Golden Mean is considered the fingerprint of creation. Your recreation of the Golden Mean sequence, particularly as it applies to your education (in a spiral manner), places you in sync with the expansion process that is at the centre of creation. It's little wonder the Golden Mean and its usage is known as 'Sacred Geometry'. In light of this knowledge, one begins to understand why Geometry is said to be the basis on which the superstructure of Freemasonry is erected, the two being synonymous.[57] The Fellowcraft Freemason is taught that Geometry is the first and noblest of sciences, and is one of the Seven Liberal Arts and Sciences, the seven being: Grammar, Rhetoric, Logic, Arithmetic, Geometry, Music, and Astronomy

As nature grows spirally, so you grow intellectually and spiritually via a spiral system. You are a part of nature, a part of all things, and therefore part of a spiralling process. This is the lesson of the Masonic winding staircase. To ascend in a spiral is not the shortest route but is the *only* route by which you truly advance. Sure, there may be a straight line shortcut but such a route is just that – an incomplete shortcut.

The winding staircase teaches that progressive education is spiral, especially from physical/material (body) to mental (mind). To reach the top of the winding stairs and enter the symbolic middle chamber – representative of the mind – requires a spiralling process we must all undertake. Short cuts (straight lines) cannot be made lest we come up short ourselves. To reach the top of the mountain your car must travel a winding road – it cannot proceed in a straight line.

The staircase's spiral composition tells you that your ascension in life must be in coherence with the laws of creation, as creation is a spiral. Ascension is only possible by conforming to the Universal Law.

Greek philosopher Aristotle wrote: 'The Universal Law is the law of Nature. For there really is, as every one to some extent divines, a natural justice and injustice that is binding on all men, even on those who have no association or covenant with each other.'[58]

The prime Universal Law states all beings are sovereign and have free will to express their creative urges in any way they choose, but no being has the right to violate and harm others. All beings, guided by the Universal Law, are prohibited from performing actions harmful to another. We should all respect the rights and boundaries of one another. It is the Golden Rule espoused by Jesus Christ to do unto others as you would have them do unto you.

Contrary to popular Christian belief, Jesus Christ was not the first sage to espouse such teaching. For as long as men have instructed in ethics, the ethic of reciprocity has existed. Confucius said: 'Never impose on others what you would not choose for yourself.'

Wrote Plato in his dialogue *Crito:* 'One should never do wrong in return, nor mistreat any man, no matter how one has been mistreated by him.'

When Hilel was asked for a summary of the teachings of the entire Torah, he answered: 'That which is hateful to you, do not do to your fellow. That is the whole Torah; the rest is the explanation; go and learn it.'[59]

The ethic of reciprocity (the Golden Rule) is a common feature of all major religions, speaking volumes for its importance. Live your life according to the Golden Rule and you cannot err.

Look at these examples of the Golden Rule found in major religions:

CHRISTIANITY
All things whatsoever ye would that men should do to you, do ye so to them; for this sums up the law and the prophets.
– Matthew 7:12

BUDDHISM
Hurt not others in ways that you yourself would find hurtful.
– Udana-Varga 5,1

HINDUISM
This is the sum of duty; do naught onto others what you would not have them do unto you.
- Mahabharata 5,1517

ISLAM
Woe to those... who, when they have to receive by measure from men, they demand exact full measure, but when they have to give by measure or weight to men, give less than due.
– Qur'an (Surah 83, The Dealers in Fraud, vv. 1–4)

TAOISM

Regard your neighbour's gain as your gain, and your neighbor's loss as your own loss.
– Tai Shang Kan Yin P'ien

ZOROASTRIANISM
That nature alone is good which refrains from doing another whatsoever is not good for itself.
– Dadisten-I-dinik, 94,5

SHINTOISM
The heart of the person before you is a mirror. See there your own form.
– Shinto Teaching

WICCA
These eight words the Rede fulfil, 'an ye harm none do as ye will.
– The Wiccan Rede

The proof of the Universal Law's existence is seen when we violate such laws, the result of which causes suffering, anguish, pain, disease, blockages, poor relationships, violence, aggression, imbalance, and the like.[60] The presence of such imbalances in your life indicates a non-conformity to the Universal Law somewhere within your make up.

The winding staircase symbolises personal progress and maturity. We cannot remain children forever. In front of us stands a winding staircase, not a straight pathway. A staircase must be climbed, and climbing is a form of labour and a means of ascension. Symbolically, therefore, the winding staircase teaches that to improve yourself, you must undertake labour and must do so in an ascending, spiral manner.

The spiral is a symbol of constant change and elevation. There is nothing stagnant about a spiral, as there should be no stagnancy is your personal advancement. It's human nature to rest on your laurels and retreat into that which is the easiest path (straight line). The spirality of the winding staircase reminds us not to be sucked into the comfort of stagnation. We must accept change, embrace it and move forward.

As Freemason Winston Churchill said, 'To improve is to change. To be perfect is to change often.'[61] If you move forward on a straight line, you never change direction. Author C. S. Lewis was correct when he said: 'It may be hard for an egg to turn into a bird: it would be a jolly sight harder for it to learn to fly while remaining an egg. We are like eggs at present. And you cannot go on indefinitely being just an ordinary, decent egg. We must be hatched or go bad.'[62]

Masonic author, Albert Mackey, writes of ascension to the middle chamber: 'It is here that the intellectual education of the candidate begins... where childhood ends and manhood begins, he finds stretching out before him a winding stair which invites him, as it were, to ascend, and which as the symbol of discipline and instruction, teaches him that here must commence Masonic labour – here he must enter upon those glorious though difficult researches, the end of which is to be the possession of divine truth...He cannot stand still if he would be worthy of his vocation; his destiny as an immortal being requires him to ascend, step by step, until the summit, where the treasures of knowledge await him.'[63]

The winding staircase is also symbolic of faith.

'Faith' is defined as *a strong belief or trust in someone or something; firm belief in something for which there is no proof: complete trust.* If you stand at the bottom of a straight staircase, you can clearly see the top. However if you stand at the bottom of a winding staircase, the top is most likely obscured from sight. It takes faith to climb towards the unknown.

Consider *The Spiral Staircase,* a spiritual short story by the late Anthony de Mello, an Indian Jesuit and psychotherapist:

'A man came upon a tall tower and stepped inside to find it all dark. As he groped around, he came upon a circular staircase. Curious to know where it led to, he began to climb, and as he climbed, he sensed a growing uneasiness in his heart.

So, he looked behind him and was horrified to see that each time he climbed a step, the previous one fell off and disappeared. Before him, the stairs wound upward and he had no idea where they led; behind him yawned an enormous black emptiness.'

Education and ascension to a higher level of being requires faith. Without faith, you will not ascend to a greater understanding of yourself and the world. Without faith in a reward for your labour at the top of the staircase, you risk descending into that enormous black emptiness of which de Mello wrote.

The white belt Karate student cannot physically see himself as a black belt. He must have faith that the system of learning he undertakes will, with the proper application of his labour, lead him to become a black belt.

You must have faith in yourself to ascend and faith in what you will find when you reach the top. As Martin Luther King Jr said: 'Faith is taking the first step even when you don't see the whole staircase.'

Have faith that in ascending your intellect through diligent labour, in accordance with the Universal Law, you will find great reward at the top of your winding staircase. Don't take shortcuts in life, especially when it comes to self-improvement. Accept that education is a spiral process, not a straight line, and ascend your own winding staircase in confidence.

Life Application

What's peculiar about standing at the foot of a winding staircase? You can't see the top. You have to have faith in the knowledge that these winding stairs will lead you to a higher place, even though you can't see that place from where you stand at the bottom.

Faith is the first lesson of the winding staircase. You must have faith that life offers a higher attainment than physical existence.

Let me relay a story of twins in a mother's womb, one who had faith of something greater than its current existence and the other who did not.

> One of the babies asked the other, 'Do you believe in life after delivery?'
>
> The other baby replied, 'Yes! There has to be more than just this, doesn't there? I think we're where we are now to prepare ourselves for life beyond delivery.'
>
> 'That's rubbish,' said the first baby. 'There is no life after delivery. I mean, what sort of life could be possible after delivery? None!'
>
> 'I don't know for sure,' said the second baby, 'but I believe there will be more light out there than in here. Perhaps we will walk on these legs we have. Maybe we'll pick up things with these arms of ours. We may be able to eat with this mouth and smell with our noses.'
>
> 'Now you're just being silly,' the first baby replied. 'Walking is impossible. And how exactly would you eat with your mouth? You know all our food comes through this cord attached to our stomachs. It's a short cord though, so logically there is no life after delivery.'
>
> 'Maybe we won't need this physical cord anymore,' said the second baby.
>
> 'Nonsense!' said the first baby. 'If there is life after delivery, why hasn't anyone ever come back from there? Delivery is the end of life. After delivery there is nothing but darkness.'
>
> 'I'm not so sure', said the second baby. 'I think after delivery we get to meet Mother and she will take care of us.'
>
> The first baby scoffed at the second baby. 'Mother? You really believe in Mother? That's ridiculous! If Mother exists, where is she now?'
>
> 'She is all around us,' answered the second baby. 'We are surrounded by her. We are part of her. We live in her. Without her this world would not exist.'
>
> 'Well, I don't see her,' huffed the first baby. 'And if I can't see her, she doesn't exist.'
>
> 'Well sometimes when it's really silent and I focus, I can feel her presence and hear her voice talking to me from above,' said the second baby.[64]

Just because you can't see the top of the winding staircase, doesn't mean the top of the staircase doesn't exist.

The winding staircase also represents education and illumination. You must have faith that education will lead you to illumination and the union of body, mind and soul to craft your highest self.

If all nature is spiral, and man is a part of nature, then man's educational process must also be spiral. Just as nature grows spirally, so do we humans grow intellectually and spiritually via a spiral system. We are a part of nature, a part of all things, and therefore part of the spiralling process. This is the lesson of the Masonic winding staircase. To ascend in a spiral is not the shortest route to the top but is the only route by which we truly advance. Sure there may be a straight line shortcut but such a route is just that – an incomplete shortcut.

Education is a lifelong process. It is imperative that you continue to educate yourself, even into old age. You may think that when you hit your seventies or eighties you've pretty much learned all there is for a lifetime. But continued education is important to keep your mind sharp.

In my own Masonic lodge and the lodges I've visited, I see many septuagenarians, octogenarians, and even some nonagenarians who remain razor sharp in their mental capacity. Why? Because Freemasonry places a major emphasis on continuous education. This is done through committing ritual to memory, including twenty-page lectures! I'm in awe watching these elderly Masons sit in lodge and silently mouth every word of the entire ritual. In addition to their amazing memory work (and it is work – hard work!) these older Masons have spent years in lodge practicing good posture, which improves blood-flow and circulation to the brain. They could have taken the straight staircase and simply adopted good posture for a few minutes while performing the particular Masonic stances and signs. But they chose to climb the winding staircase, diligently disciplining their bodies at every lodge meeting for decades to reap this invaluable reward for their labour.

Good posture was developed by these men through the cultivation of good habits. Good habits do not form overnight. There is no shortcut to forming habits that improve your lifestyle. Researchers believe it takes 21 days for neural pathways to form in the brain and create a new habit.

A long held Masonic 'secret' is the development of positive habits through the practice of repeated actions. Doing the same positive action over and over again – without shortcuts – establishes and strengthens the neural pathways.

Although you can't see the top of the staircase (the new habit) when standing at the bottom (the decision to form a new habit), have faith in the knowledge of the fact that through diligent practice without shortcuts (climbing the winding staircase) new habits form that will positively affect your life.

Ask Yourself
- Have I stagnated in my education or am I continuing to learn new things?
- Am I advancing my intelligence in a spiralling ascension or moving in a straight line?
- Is my increased materialism negatively affecting my intellectual advancement?
- Do I feel in touch with nature or out of synch with the movement of all around me?
- Is there anyone in my life who is preventing me from ascending my own winding staircase?
- I work out to train my body but do I train my mind?
- Am I constantly looking for short cuts to success (straight road) and not realising that success is the result of diligent labour (winding staircase)?
- Is my current system of learning (be it at work, at school, in Karate or yoga class, online, etc.) offering me the proper method for self-betterment?
- What do I expect to find when I reach the top of my own winding staircase?

Black and white
The mosaic pavement

One should see the world, and see himself as a scale with an equal balance of good and evil.

— Maimonides

A black and white checkered pavement adorns the centre of most Masonic lodge rooms. Known as the mosaic pavement or checkered floorboard, it is a symbol rich with significance and ancient in its usage.

The mosaic pavement is one of the three ornaments of a lodge, the other two being the tessellated border surrounding the pavement and the blazing star at its centre. All three ornaments may be grouped together as one overall symbol. We are going to concentrate on the mosaic pavement, which is loaded with symbolism of a concept that has existed since the very moment of creation.

Freemasonry teaches that the mosaic pavement represents the ground floor of King Solomon's Temple and is emblematic of human life being checkered with good and evil. That's it!

This explanation is far too minimalistic for such a widely used symbol, but the essence is correct. Human life *is* checkered with good and evil. It is also checkered with light and dark; up and down; in and out; anger and sadness; joy and despair; left and right; positive and negative; speed and slowness; strength and weakness; men and women; memory and forgetfulness – you get the picture. Everything in life has its opposite. Nothing exists as a singleness. Duality is all about us, and is symbolised by the mosaic pavement.

According to the Book of Genesis, when God created the Earth, he separated light from darkness. Thus, duality began from the very moment of creation. God went on to accomplish more cool feats of duality. He separated the earth from heaven and made a light for the day and a light for the night. On the sixth day of creation, God created the duality of man (Genesis 1:27).

Whoa, you may be thinking. God didn't make two men. He made one man named Adam then he made a woman named Eve to keep Adam company. That's Old Testament 101!

Examine the words of Genesis 1:27 closely:

'God created man in His own image, in the image of God He created him; male and female…'

Where does it say God created an actual, physical woman at this stage? Genesis states later in Chapter 2:21-22 that God created a woman (Eve) out of one of Adam's ribs. However, where is the mention of Eve's creation earlier in Genesis 1:27?

If 'male and female He created them' doesn't actually mean the separate creation of a man and a woman, what does it mean?

According to Joseph B. Soloveitchik (1903-1993) an influential American rabbi, Talmudist, and modern Jewish philosopher, Genesis 1:27 does not refer to man's physical composition but to his psychological make up. 'Male and female' represents man's psychological tendencies; namely active and progressive – the duality of man's nature.'[65]

Duality therefore can be traced back to the creation of man. Fast forward a few millennia and we see the concept symbolised in cultures and belief systems across the world. The mosaic pavement of Freemasonry is but one well-known representation of duality but not the most renowned. That privilege belongs to the yin and yang.

The yin and yang symbol, known as the Taijitu, translates as 'diagram of the supreme ultimate' and 'great polarity'. It looks like two fish chasing one another inside a round. You've most likely seen a version of it, known as a Taeguk, on the South Korean flag.

The colours of a true Taijitu are black and white (mosaic pavement anyone?). Yin is the black side with a white dot in it, and yang is the white side with a black dot in it. The same pattern can also be found in ancient Roman, Celtic, Etruscan, and Cucuteni-Trypillian culture (4800 - 3000 BCE), and offers an indication as to the antiquity of the symbol. The earliest reference to yin and yang dates to around 700

BCE, and is found in the *I Ching* (Book of Changes) in which all phenomena are said to be reduced to yin and yang.

What does it all mean and why is the Taijitu called the 'supreme ultimate'?

Yin and yang, like the mosaic pavement, is symbolic of contrary forces in the physical world, and how they're interdependent on one another. Opposites in nature are complementary of one another. Light cannot exist without darkness; good cannot exist without evil; there is no up without down and there is no woman without man (that rib from Adam, remember?). Wrote Lao Tzu in the *Tao Te Ching*:

'When people see things as beautiful,
ugliness is created.
When people see things as good,
evil is created.
Being and non-being produce each other.
Difficult and easy complement each other.
Long and short define each other.
High and low oppose each other.
Fore and aft follow each other.'

The key to living in a world of dichotomies is to find balance therein – a balance between cause and consequence. This is the Socratic law of causality, so profound and powerful that is has been referred to as the 'Iron Law of Human Destiny'. It is Sir Isaac Newton's third law of motion, which states: 'for every action, there is an equal and opposite reaction.'

Think of the dualities of your life as a circuit, as a flow. The dualities travel in the opposite direction (up and down, left and right) and create a flow that travels around the very centre of yourself. Consider dualities as a battery with a negative charge and a positive charge. When these two charges are balanced, again, a balance between cause and consequence, the result is an electrical charge which is the harmony of these two opposing (+ / -) forces, or dualities. The key to activating a battery's power supply is to equally charge the negative and the positive – to strike balance. A power socket relies on input and output. Too much of one or the other will cause the power socket to blow. A balance must be attained between the input and output – between the dualities – to achieve the proper flow of power.

Your life is not etched in stone. Every aspect of your existence is within your means to change if you impress the correct actions upon your life. Wrote Newton in *The Principia: Mathematical Principles of Natural Philosophy:* 'Impressed force is the action exerted on a body to change its state either of resting or of moving uniformly straight forward.'

You have the power to change yourself.

Relative levels of yin and yang are continuously varying. When either yin or yang is out of balance, they affect each other. Too much yin or too little yang can eventually weaken the other. The challenge is to balance your yin and yang.

How often have you heard somebody say they feel 'out of whack' or 'I'm not myself today'? This is a good sign that the person is walking on more black squares than white squares on the mosaic pavement of their life.

Our personalities comprise two polar opposites: our male and female nature, dynamic and passive. These are the two poles of human behaviour – the yin and yang, good and evil, brutish and enlightened, emotional and reasonable, human and godly – found in each and every one of us.

Learning to keep yourself in balance between the two poles is difficult, but achievable. In our struggle to do good, we're eternally at war against our material pleasures. A boxing promoter may bill it as: God versus Satan in a fight for your soul. Shakespeare put it a little more eloquently when he wrote: 'The web of our life is a mingled yarn, good and ill together.'

Hermetic philosophy details Seven Principles by which the entire universe is governed. This philosophy is said to be the essence of the teachings of Hermes Trismegistus (thrice-great Hermes), the purported author of the *Hermetic Corpus*, a series of sacred texts that are the basis of Hermeticism. It is debated as to whether Hermes was, in fact, Greek or Egyptian and whether or not he was an actual physical person at all or rather a conscious energy construct without a body. Interestingly, the celebrated American psychic, Edgar Cayce, claimed in some of his trance readings that Hermes or Thoth (the Egyptian moon good) was an engineer from the submerged Atlantis, who also built, designed or directed the construction of the Pyramids of Egypt.[66]

The writings of Hermes Trismegistus enjoyed a revival during the Middle Ages and the Renaissance. With the development of speculative Freemasonry during the latter, it is easy to see how aspects of Hermetic philosophy may have impacted Masonic teaching and ritual.

The Seven Hermetic Principles are:

1. The Principle of Mentalism – the belief that all is mind, the universe is mental.
2. The Principle of Correspondence – As above, so below. There is always a correspondence between the various planes of existence.
3. The Principle of Vibration – Everything is in motion, nothing rests.

4. The Principle of Polarity – Everything is dual. Everything has its pair of opposites.
5. The Principle of Rhythm – All things rise and fall. Everything goes in and out.
6. The Principle of Cause and Effect – Every cause has its effect. Everything happens according to law and nothing is by chance.
7. The Principle of Gender – Masculine and feminine manifests on all planes.

The mosaic pavement is symbolic of the Principle of Polarity. The unknown authors of *The Kybalion*[67] wrote: 'Everything is Dual; everything has poles; everything has its pair of opposites; like and unlike are the same; opposites are identical in nature, but different in degree; extremes meet; all truths are but half-truths; all paradoxes may be reconciled.'

As everything has its two poles, then 'good and evil' are but the poles of the same thing. Same, too, with 'love and hate.' Hermeticism teaches that through the Art of Polarisation, a form of mental alchemy, we can transmute evil into good. It is only when one understands the Principle of Polarity that one can begin to change one's own polarity, and the polarity of others through the changing of vibrations in the mind.

Sounds a little hokey, you may be thinking. Let's simplify it a little more.

If all is energy, then your thoughts are a form of energy. If energy is vibration, then your thoughts are vibrations. If you think hatred towards another person, your thought emits a certain type of vibration like striking a minor chord on a piano. If you think thoughts of love towards the same person, you effectively change the vibration of your thoughts – you move the fingers from a minor chord to a more melodic major chord. You recognise the negative vibration (the pole of hate) and transmute it into a positive vibration (the pole of love).

Vibrational frequency is the rate of vibration of the atoms and sub-particles in a being or object. Our words and thoughts emit lower or higher frequency vibrations that attract like vibrations.[68] Hate attracts hate; peace attracts peace; love attracts love; fear attracts fear.

Similarly, we are attracted to people who operate near to the same frequency we resonate. This is why in certain social settings you may feel 'out of place' or 'uncomfortable' or 'out of your comfort zone' being around people who are not resonating on a similar vibrational frequency.

You are capable of changing the vibrational frequency of your thoughts to change yourself and your surroundings. Let me give you an example.

My wife recently told me a story about how she managed to change the vibration of her thoughts to overcome a fear of flying. While my wife was pregnant, we traveled from Australia to the United States, which is a 15-hour flight aboard a massive Air Bus A380. With every bump of turbulence, and every fall and rise in altitude, my wife would go stiff as a plank. She would usually take a pill to calm her nerves but being pregnant she wasn't allowed to do so. Moreover, it turns out, she didn't need a pill. All she needed was a shift in the vibration of her thoughts. She transmuted her paralysing thoughts of fear into thoughts of joy and became a lot more relaxed on this marathon flight. How did she do it? Here's what she told me:

'I thought to myself, if a natural disaster happens, like an earthquake or a tsunami, where is the place I would like to be? Safe in this plane. The airplane would be my rescue. The airplane would be my saving grace. So instead of being scared to fly I concentrated on a reason why I would be relieved and happy to be flying, and I calmed down. I didn't need to take a pill. The fear went away.'

A little bit of positive thinking allowed my wife to move her mental fingers from a minor chord to a major chord. She recognised the negative vibration (the pole of anxiety) and transmuted it into a positive vibration (the pole of calmness). She recognised the duality, the opposites, and used this knowledge to her advantage. Anxiety doesn't exist without calmness just as calmness doesn't exist without anxiety.

John K. Johnston wrote: 'The dualism of these opposites governs us in everything, and experience of it is prescribed for us until such time as, having learned and outgrown its lesson, we are ready for advancement to a condition where we outgrow the sense of this chequer-work existence and those opposites cease to be perceived as opposites, but are realised as a unity or synthesis.'[69]

The placement of the mosaic pavement is also symbolic. That the pavement is located on the floor and not on the ceiling, or the wall, symbolises that it is something to be walked on. The ground provides the foundation for us to walk on, which we must do as just and upright beings. That is, we should endeavour to keep our head high, our shoulders straight and stay perfectly balanced on the mosaic pavement of life. Being balanced, literally and figuratively, begins from the feet up.

At the centre of the mosaic pavement sits the blazing star. This is our reward for a balanced life. Just as you received a gold star for homework well done in school, so a job well done in balancing life – body (material), mind (mental), soul (spiritual) – will reward you with a blazing star, symbolic of the divinity at your centre, your eternal soul. This is, after all, the great quest of all schools of learning, particularly Freemasonry. Said Cicero (106-43 BCE): 'The establishment of these rites among the Athenians conferred upon them a supreme benefit. Their effect was to civilise man, reform their wild and ferocious manners, and make them comprehend the true principles of morality, which initiate man into a new order of life, more worthy of a being destined to immortality.'[70]

Finding the balance between your inner Dr Jekyll and Mr Hyde, your inner Bruce Banner and The Incredible Hulk, your inner Bruce Wayne and Batman, your positive and negative battery charge, is the challenge of walking the mosaic pavement that covers the flooring of your life; flooring on which we all must walk. Once you accept this fact and embrace it, the effect lessens.

What you think manifests physically. A perfectly balanced state of mind leads to a perfect objective manifestation in the body and your surroundings. When your mind is unbalanced, out of whack, more yang than yin, you will manifest forms and ways that are detrimental not just to yourself, but to all around you.

Life Application
Do you feel a sense of harmony within yourself or are you split by dualities? Can you identify the dualities of your personality and the prominent dualities in your life?

Your physical existence is full of dualities. It is important to recognise the dualities both in yourself and in your surroundings, and examine whether you resist these dualities or embrace them.

Life is never stagnant. You are always heading in a direction. When you feel like life is going nowhere, understand this: you are always heading in a direction, albeit sometimes not the direction you want to take. Also, remember: you can change direction at any time.

Question what course your life is currently taking and the dualities of that course. Are you pleased with life's course? If the answer is no, then know that you alone have the power to change direction. You alone have the power to shift your mental fingers from a minor chord to a major chord. You alone have the power to step off the 'black squares' of your mosaic pavement and hop onto the 'white squares'.

If life isn't going the way you hoped, try sourcing the cause of your current course of action, and the effect of the cause. Take a step from the black squares to the white squares by transmuting your negative thoughts into positive thoughts; your thoughts of hate into thoughts of love. Remember all is energy and you can change your energy – your vibrations – and affect a more positive heart and mind. When you accept that black cannot exist without white, good cannot exist without evil; up cannot exist without down, you can move onto changing the polarities in your life.

Hermeticism teaches that through the Art of Polarisation, a form of mental alchemy, you can transmute evil into good. It is only when one understands the Principle of Polarity – represented by the Mosaic pavement of Freemasonry – that one can begin to change one's own polarity, and the polarity of others through the changing of mental vibrational frequency.

Ask Yourself
- Am I in harmony or am I split by dualities?
- What are the dualities most prominent in my life?
- What are the dualities of my personality?
- Do I resist the dualities of my personality or embrace them?
- What are the dualities of a current course of action I am taking in my life?
- Am I pleased with my current course of action?
- What choices can I make to alter my current course of action and bring my life into greater balance?
- What is the cause of my current course of action?
- What is the desired effect of my current course of action?
- In my actions today did I step on more black squares or white squares?
- Do I harbour hateful thoughts towards another person?
- How can I transmute my hateful thoughts into thoughts of love?
- In what other aspects of my life can I change my energy – my vibrations – and effect a more positive mind and heart?
- What polarises me?

Sssh!
Silence and secrecy

See how nature – trees, flowers, grass – grows in silence;
see the stars, the moon and the sun, how they move in silence…
We need silence to be able to touch souls.

— Mother Teresa

Silence and secrecy form the backbone of Masonic instruction and are two of the most debated, despised, and misunderstood aspects of Freemasonry in the eyes of the general public.

Let's get one thing straight from the outset: Freemasonry is not a secret society. If it *was* a secret society, this book would not be in publication. If it was a secret society, its membership would be concealed and its meeting places unadorned with its very non-secret square and compasses.

If Freemasonry was a secret society, its members would not participate in public parades, and there would be no Freemasons Hospitals or Shriners Hospitals. A secret society would not provide scholarship programs such as the one conducted by the Grand Lodge of Iowa, which sponsors sixty annual scholarship awards for post-secondary education.

If Freemasonry was a secret society, it would not be prevalent in such Hollywood films as *The Man Who Would Be King* (Sean Connery, Michael Caine, Christopher Plummer), based on a story by Rudyard Kipling, himself a Freemason initiated into Hope and Perseverance Lodge No.782 in Lahore, India.

Other Hollywood films featuring aspects of Freemasonry include: *Paper Moon, Rosewood, National Treasure, Tombstone, Prisoners, The League of Extraordinary Gentlemen, Erin Brockovich,* and *Magnolia.*

It is commonly said that Freemasonry is not a secret society but is a society with secrets. A more apt saying is that Freemasonry is not a secret society but is a society with *secrecy*. Freemasonry doesn't promote secrets but it does adjure secrecy. You're about to understand why.

Silence and secrecy are among the first lessons taught to a Freemason and are reiterated consistently throughout its solemn obligations. An ivory key is often used as a symbol of silence and secrecy, as is seen in some versions of the First Degree

Tracing Board and is prevalent in the Fourth Degree of Secret Master of the Ancient and Accepted Scottish Rite.

A symbol of ancient origin, the key is found in various teaching systems throughout many cultures, including the mystery schools of Ancient Egypt and Greece, the Romans, Hebrews, and Christians.

The need for secrecy and silence is sternly imparted upon the candidate from his first step into the lodge room. There is nothing secret or silent about the manner in which a new Mason is drilled with the exhortation to keep his mouth shut.

You may ask, *So why are Masons so secretive?*

Before answering that question, let's examine the difference between silence and secrecy.

Silence is defined as *a lack of sound or noise; a situation, state, or period of time in which people do not talk; a situation or state in which someone does not talk about or answer questions about anything.*

One can be silent without being secret; silence requires no secrecy, it only requires no sound.

What then is secrecy?

Secrecy is defined as *the condition of being hidden or concealed; the habit or practice of keeping secrets or maintaining privacy or concealment.*

Hence, silence and secrecy, though seemingly connected on the surface, are wholly different ideas. A friend may talk about how much money he makes at his job, but will hold secret the real amount in his pay-cheque. KFC waxes lyrical about the taste of its chicken, but will keep hidden its eleven secret herbs and spices.

The Masonic key is said to represent the tongue, which should speak well of a brother absent or present. Masons are taught that when one cannot speak well of another, one should adopt that 'excellent virtue of the Craft' which is silence. At its most basic, therefore, the key is an apt symbol for locking something important in a place inaccessible to those without permission to gain access.

That the key is fashioned from ivory and not metal presents a further explanation of the symbol. Ivory is a bone derived from the tusks and teeth of animals, in particular the tusks of an elephant. The key is symbolic of the tongue inside the skull where it is protected by the teeth (ivory bones).

In the early Masonic lectures of the eighteenth century, we find the following catechism[71]:

Q: Have you any key to the secrets of a Mason?
A: Yes.
Q: Where do you keep it?

A: In a bone box, that neither opens nor shuts but with ivory keys.

The bone box here clearly refers to the mouth and the ivory keys to the teeth. The act of speaking, which is how secrets are conveyed, is performed by opening one's mouth (bone box) and teeth (ivory keys). The tongue is the key to the secrets of Freemasonry. By its use we are able to convey the knowledge of the Craft. By closing the mouth and locking up the tongue, we are able to protect that knowledge. Among the ancients, the key was considered a symbol of silence, secrecy, and circumspection.[72]

The symbolic key features in various Bible verses. Isaiah 22:22 states:

And the key of the house of David will I lay upon his shoulder; so he shall open, and none shall shut; and he shall shut, and none shall open.[73]

Scholars speculate that the key laid upon the shoulder refers to an ancient ceremony of placing keys on the shoulder of an officer of the state to signify his power. I believe the explanation of this passage is far simpler and of greater symbolism.

What part of the body is placed on the shoulders? The head.

What does the head house? The mouth.

What does the mouth hold? The tongue.

What does the tongue do? It either talks or keeps quiet.

The tongue conveys teachings, imparts wisdom, speaks secrets and also locks up secrets. Each of us has the power to open our mouth (he shall open) and when our mouth is open nobody has the power to shut it (none shall shut). When we shut our mouths (and he shall shut) nobody has the power to open our mouths (and none shall open). Our ivory key gives us the power to communicate the treasures of the world, to relay greater knowledge or to keep such knowledge secret.

The Masonic key teaches that we alone have the power to give or deny our secrets to others. Creation placed the key of the house of David upon the shoulders, that is, in our head where the brain is located, and from which our earthly intelligence emanates. Should the brain tell the mouth to divulge a secret, the mouth will oblige.

In Matthew 16:9 Jesus says: 'I will give you the keys of the kingdom of heaven; whatever you bind on earth will be bound in heaven, and whatever you loose on earth will be loosed in heaven'.[74]

The 'keys to the kingdom of heaven' is the knowledge of how to reconnect with your centre. At this centre is your divine spark, the place from which your soul originates. It is pure energy. Heaven is not a physical place among the clouds where angels strum harps and Elvis Presley drinks cocktails at the bar with James Dean. Heaven is a state of being, achieved by reaching a level of consciousness where physical manifestation is no longer required – dominion of the soul. Achievement of this level of consciousness is the highest teaching of almost every instructional organisation, from the great religions of the world to the ancient mystery schools.

Writes Major R. Watkins-Pitchford: 'The main purpose of the allegories and symbols employed in Freemasonry is to induce the Candidate to recognise the spiritual nature imminent within himself, to develop this spiritual nature into a fuller conscious co-operation with its Author, and, above all, to achieve that balance between body and mind which is essential to spiritual advancement.'[75]

Jesus offers knowledge veiled in allegory, using parables about how to live one's life so as to prepare for post-mortem existence. In Matthew 16:9 Jesus tells us that what we sew on earth, we reap in heaven (as above, so below). Be careful what you say, choose your words wisely and use the keys of knowledge sagely because whatever you bind on earth will be bound in heaven – you become (earth) what you think (heaven).

Whoa! Hold on a moment, you may be thinking. *You're talking about Jesus and David and elephant tusks and tongues. What about the secrecy stuff? Why is secrecy and silence so important to Freemasons?*

Secrecy and silence are not exclusive to Masonic teaching; there exists more silent history of the world than that which is spoken.

Wellins Calcott, author of *A Candid Disquisition of the Principles and Practices of the Most Ancient and Honorable Society of Free and Accepted Masons* (quite possibly the longest book title ever), wrote of the ancient veneration of secrecy and silence: '… we shall find that the old Egyptians had so great a regard for silence and secrecy in the mysteries of their religion, that they set up the god Harpocrates, to whom they paid peculiar honour and veneration, who was represented with the right hand placed near the heart, and the left down by his side, covered with a skin before, full of eyes and ears, to signify, that of many things to be seen and heard, few are to be published.'[76]

Apuleius (124 CE-170 CE), a Platonic philosopher who was an initiate in the Mysteries of Isis, said: 'By no peril will I ever be compelled to disclose to the uninitiated the things that I have had entrusted to me on condition of silence.'[77]

The best-known champion of silence and secrecy was Pythagoras. To become a member of the Pythagorean School, an initiate took an oath of silence for two to five years. Novices were called 'Listeners' and were not permitted to partake in class discussions, but only to listen so the teaching could be absorbed before entering into an intellectual debate on what they learned.

Said Pythagoras: 'It is better wither to be silent, or to say things of more value than silence. Sooner throw a pearl at hazard than an idle or useless word; and do not say a little in many words, but a great deal in a few.'

Silence was a discipline of the Pythagorean community later inherited by the Essenes and Therapeutic communities. In Turkey, students of the Mevlevi School of Dervishes spent as much as three years in silence to induce changes in states of consciousness before becoming full initiates.

Saint Symeon, the New Theologian (949-1022 CE), was a Byzantine Christian monk and poet who was the last of three saints canonised by the Eastern Orthodox Church.[78] One of his major teachings was that we are all capable of *theoria*, or a direct experience of God. Indeed the word Theologian in the days of Saint Symeon referred to one who experienced God directly, one-on-one.

Saint Symeon achieved theoria by the lifelong practice of hesychia. Derived from the Greek work *hesychasmos*, meaning 'stillness, rest, calmness, silence', hesychia is a form of prayer directed inwards through a total stilling of the senses, and a silence of the heart. It is based on the words of Jesus in Matthew 6:6: 'When thou prayest, enter into thy closet, and when thou has shut thy door, pray.'

Let me stress here that the action of praying, which Saint Symeon and Jesus talk about, does not necessarily mean praying to God or the saints. Prayer is a form of meditation. It is a form of focusing, of quieting the mind, stilling the body and centering oneself. You do not have to be of a religious inclination to reap the benefits of prayer when it is understood in this way. I've met yoga practitioners, martial artists, dancers, actors, athletes, and entrepreneurs who use meditation to go within themselves and connect with their centre.

The martial artists I have spoken to consider silent meditation as a manipulation of energy. Through meditation, they increase awareness, focus and calmness – three important aspects also required to win a physical battle. As a long-time combat sports broadcaster, I have commentated more than five-thousand fights on television and know that the most successful fighters in boxing, mixed martial arts and kickboxing all have three traits in common: awareness, focus and calmness. Awareness allows a fighter to anticipate attacks; focus allows a fighter to react to those attacks accordingly; calmness allows a fighter to relax and centre his attack/defence, so as to not expel unnecessary energy. Silence (prayer, meditation) allows one to go-inside oneself and achieve greater awareness, focus and calmness, which brings about enhanced clarity for dealing with life's situations.

To establish the true necessity for silence and secrecy in your life, it is necessary to once again treat each as a separate idea.

Let's examine the importance of secrecy.

Here we go, you may be thinking. Now for the juicy stuff! UFO cover-ups; who killed JFK; the Illuminati agenda; an explanation of the final episode of LOST – all the good stuff you Freemasons keep secret!

Conspiracy theorists eager for the divulgence of such information will be sorely disappointed. Masons do not take (multiple) obligations of secrecy to cover up any such knowledge. The necessity for secrecy in Masonry is the same as the necessity for secrecy in daily life: to build character.

An old Greek philosopher, when asked what he regarded as the most valuable quality to win, and the most difficult to keep, replied: 'To be secret and silent.'[79] Keeping a secret requires a strong mental state. We have a natural urge to tell others what we know. Think for a moment how much of your own talking time is taken up by idle conversation and useless (perhaps even harmful) gossip. A person capable of keeping a secret – of keeping their mouth shut – boasts a greater moral character than one who cannot keep a secret. A gentleman has always been judged by his manner of speech. If Masonry's aim is to 'make good men better', then developing the ability to keep a secret is of the utmost importance.

'Secrecy is the ability to keep a confidence,' writes 33rd degree Mason, Jim Tresner,[80] 'Great systems of philosophy have taught through the ages that such ability is the first step in developing self-discipline and self-control.' He who routinely 'spills the beans' when asked to keep a secret, exercises no self-control. Without self-control, without discipline and willpower, we cannot improve our lives. Through self-control we ascend the winding staircase, and through willpower we use the common gavel to smooth our rough edges.

Daniel Sickels writes in the 1867 book, *The General Ahiman Rezon and Freemasons Guide*: 'Another reason why Freemasonry regards secrecy as a fundamental principle is because a unity, harmony and strength can be secured thereby, which cannot be obtained in any other way. Secrecy has a mystic, binding, almost supernatural force, and unites men more closely together than all other means combined. The common possession of a secret by a considerable number of people produces a family feeling.'

If, as Plato says, the design of initiation is to restore the soul to that state of perfection from which it had originally fallen, then secrecy, which contributes to the development of self-discipline, is integral to this end goal.

We keep secrets in our hearts, locked by our intelligence with the key of willpower. So long as the lock and key are in good working condition, a safe cannot be broken into. What we value we instinctively guard.[81]

Knowing when to talk and when to 'bite your tongue' is an imperative part of building character. It was Krishna who said: 'If you are able to regulate your tongue, 70 per cent of your spiritual practice is complete.'

This brings us to the topic of silence. Silence is not the absence of words but the stilling of the mind. Silence, it is said, is the playground of the gods. It is through stillness of the mind that we are able to connect with our centre.

Silence is achieved through meditation. How you should meditate is for your own discovery. Some methods of meditation include yoga, martial arts, prayer, breathing exercises or traditional meditation techniques such as mantra meditation. Others find the benefits of meditation – stilling the mind – through engrossing activities such as cooking, reading, running, cycling, walking or fishing. Once found and employed in your daily life, silencing your mind will increase brain wave coherence and contribute to improved memory retrieval, attention span, creativity, and learning abilities. The practice of silencing the mind also contributes to reduced anxiety and lowered blood pressure.

Life is full of noise. The buzzing phone, honking car horn, humming refrigerator, babbling television, hissing soda can, and that annoying *swoop* sound made when someone messages you on Skype, all form the score of your material existence. There's nothing wrong with the material – it is part and parcel of being human – but you do have a choice to aspire to something higher. You have the choice to find silence and improve your internal qualities ahead of improving your external self. You can choose to reconnect with your centre and be more than what you see in the mirror.

Meister Eckhart (1260-1328 CE), a German theologian, philosopher and mystic, said: 'There is nothing so much like God as silence.'

Mother Teresa insisted on two hours of silent prayer a day and said: 'Silence is God speaking to us.'

Silence allows us to experience and understand that which we cannot while connected to the interferences of the material world. Take the story of a group of rabbinical students who were debating the meaning of a biblical text. Asking their teacher to intervene, the teacher pointed at the page and asked, 'What do you see here?' The students replied, 'The text we've been arguing about.' The teacher pointed to the words on the page and said, 'These black marks on the page contain half the meaning of the passage. The other half is in the white spaces between the words.'[82]

The ink on the pages of your life is your material existence. You can learn a lot in this existence: achieve doctorates, write books and hang certificates on the wall. But around the black marks are the white spaces of elevated learning, which are attained when the words made by the black marks are silenced.

Consider the following quote about Freemasonry: 'In the quiet of the tyled lodge, shut away from the noise and clatter of the world, in an air of reverence and friendship, it teaches us the truths that make us men, upon which faith and character must rest if they are to endure the wind and weather of life.'[83]

With the knowledge attained in previous chapters, understanding that the lodge is symbolic of a person, examine this sentence again with my explanation in parentheses and how it relates to your life.

> 'In the quiet of the tyled lodge (in the quiet of your mind), shut away from the noise and clatter of the world (in a state of silence, focused internally and closed to interferences of the material world), in an air of reverence and friendship (whereby you have achieved a sense of harmony within yourself, that is, at peace with yourself as you would be with good friends), it (silence or inner focus) teaches us the truths that make us men (allows us to study ourselves, analyse our make up and detect areas of improvement) upon which faith and character must rest (that are vital to our mental and spiritual growth) if they are to endure the weather of life (if we are going to elevate ourselves above a mere material existence).'

In the movie *Happy Gilmore,* Happy, a hockey player turned pro golfer, initially struggles to putt a golf ball. After Happy violently vents his anger on a mini-golf course, golf pro Chubbs teaches Happy to find his happy place whenever overwhelmed by feelings of anger and frustration. Chubbs says, 'Remember this isn't hockey, you don't play with raw emotion. You can't putt angry. You have to clear your mind of everything else and stay focused. Think of a place that's really perfect. Your own happy place. Go there and all your anger will just disappear. Then putt.'

Happy silences his mind through a form of meditation in which he visualises his grandmother playing slot machines, a dwarf cowboy riding a tricycle, and a woman clad in lingerie serving jugs of beer. Through achieving stillness of the mind and silencing the deafening noise of the material world, Happy is empowered with clarity, focus, calmness and the ability to putt the ball.

The silence of the mind allows you to plug into the unmanifest; the divine spark within. As Psalm 46:10 tells us: 'Be still and know.' Just as Happy Gilmore stills his mind to find his happy place and achieve success, once you develop the ability to create a state of silence, you will be able to invoke it in any scenario – even when playing mini-golf.

Life Application
Can you keep a secret?
    Are you trustworthy?
    Is your character reliable enough for someone to entrust you with their secrets?
    Secrecy gets a bad rap these days, but in ancient times it was considered an important character trait. Consider for a moment how much talking time is consumed

by idle gossip instead of quality conversation. Gossip gets you nowhere closer to reconnecting with your higher self. It is better to remain silent than to gossip about others.

Consider this passage from James 3:5: 'Our tongues are small and yet they boast about big things...the tongue is like a spark. It takes only a spark to start a forest fire. It is an evil power that can soil the rest of the body and sets a person's entire life on fire with flames that come from the infernal regions...My dear friends, with our tongues we speak both praises and curses. We praise our God and Father and we speak evil of folk who were created to be like God, and that is not right.'

Human nature rejects change and protests internalisation of new knowledge because we have been programmed our entire lives to think and act differently. You once thought within the limitations of material/physical experiences but as you have seen through the lessons presented in this book, there is a whole other reality in which you exist – the spiritual reality.

One of the greatest roadblocks to internalisation of new knowledge is the desire to discuss this knowledge with everyone. I strongly advise against such practice. You don't need validation from others, you need only know the benefits this knowledge offers you and how you can apply this knowledge to better yourself. The moment you begin telling the world about your newfound knowledge is the moment you miss the point of acquiring this knowledge. Shouting about something new from the rooftops may seem like a good idea, but it is not proof of practice.

You don't need validation from the masses. External responses are not sought here; it is internalisation of what you have learnt that is important. Understand this and you will understand why silence and secrecy are so important in the internalisation process. It is the internal and not the external qualities of a man Freemasonry regards.

Resisting the urge to externalise your newfound knowledge will help you develop the self-confidence to not seek validation from others. The only approval you need should come from within. Remember, nobody will ever have the level of zeal for your improvement that you have for yourself.

Ask Yourself
- When was the last time someone asked me to keep a secret? Did I keep it?
- Who do I trust enough to confide my secrets?
- Am I trustworthy?
- When was the last time I experienced true silence?
- If I sit in silence and focus inward, what will I see?
- What activities can I do which will promote a state of silence?

- Do I really hear people when they talk or do I only listen until I can speak?
- Where is my happy place?

The Universe's Google
The pencil

Your beliefs become your thoughts,
Your thoughts become your words,
Your words become your actions,
Your actions become your habits,
Your habits become your values,
Your values become your destiny.

— Mohandas Karamchand "Mahatma" Gandhi

The Third Degree of Freemasonry, known as the Sublime Degree of Master Mason, presents three working tools to the newly made Master Mason[84]: the compasses, the skirrett and the pencil.

You may be thinking, *the pencil? Really? That's some kind of knowledge-filled working tool? Is a standard yellow HB pencil okay? Does it need an eraser?*

That a simple pencil is a working tool of the highest degree of Freemasonry sounds ludicrous, right? Surely there's no deep insight to be garnered from a pencil? You write with it – that's all!

On face value, the pencil seems like a working tool you wouldn't expect the sages and adepts of old to have embedded with symbolism. It's hard to imagine Pythagoras or Confucius holding a pencil to the heavens, proclaiming they'd found the secret of life, and admonishing their followers to keep their pencils sharpened. However, the meaning behind this simplest of working tools is rich and complex. It pertains to every one of us; every thought we have and every action we perform, every moment of every hour of our lives. Given that the average human life lasts around 613,000 hours, that's a lot to write about!

A second-by-second diary of your current thought process may look something like this:

- Reading page 118 of this book
- Thinking of a yellow HB pencil with an eraser
- Picturing Socrates wielding a pencil
- Thinking my pencil is sharpened nicely

- My finger hurts when I write
- Guess we don't write so much anymore as we type
- Can I still write cursive? Let me take a break from reading and write by hand
- Hey, my cursive isn't too bad!
- Turning the page of this book
- Reading more words
- What am I going to have for lunch?
- A burger would be nice
- I haven't had a burger for a couple of weeks
- There's a McDonald's just down the road
- I'll have a cheeseburger and fries
- And a shake
- Chocolate shake
- Vanilla
- Chocolate
- Okay, what was I reading
- Oh yeah, uh huh, stuff about a pencil

You've just covered your thought process for the last ten seconds. Apparently, the average human mind has about 63,000 thoughts a day – that's almost 44 thoughts a minute. If you're a high thinker, a procrastinator, a worrier or a Candy Crush addict, the number of thoughts per day would be exponentially more.

Social media is an intriguing indicator as to what we are all thinking. Consider that every Tweet or Facebook status is one of those 63,000 thoughts you average in a day. Facebook receives about 700 status updates per second. Twitter receives around 600 tweets per second. Google averages 34,000 searches per second.[85] It's amazing how many thoughts we have! Add action to each of those thoughts and you see how we human beings are in constant motion, both in mind and body.

After we think, where do our thoughts go? Do they evaporate, cease to exist or live on somehow, somewhere?

Albert Einstein said, 'Energy cannot be created or destroyed, it can only be changed from one form to another.' This is known as the Law of Conservation of Energy. Interesting, isn't it? So, if energy can't be destroyed, and our thoughts are energy, it serves to reason that once we think, those thoughts must exist forever, right?

By the same reasoning our actions, which are also energy, are never destroyed. We know that an action once performed can never be reversed. We are unable to go back in time and undo the actions we have done. Every action affects another action, and that action in turn affects another action, and so on. Once the second is lived, it is never lived again. Our entire lives are a consequence of every action performed, all of which are irreversible.

Simply put, once you think a thought and once you perform an action, that thought and action are made forever. There's no turning back. Says American preacher and Christian writer, Edwin Hubbell Chapin: 'Every action of our lives touches on some chord that will vibrate in eternity.'

Let me demonstrate further the irreversibility of thought.

Think of the colour blue.

Now think of the colour yellow.

Can you go back and change the original blue thought into a thought of purple or green? No. You can have a different thought of purple or green but you cannot reverse the previous thought.

Turn the page of this book then turn it back again.

Your continued reading is a succeeding action of turning the page back to where it was. You can't go back and not turn the page you turned earlier. You may perform a different action now and not turn the page again, but your previous action of turning the page when asked of you will never be undone.

Every thought and action is irreversible.

If thought and action are irreversible and are forms of energy, which is never destroyed, then they are recorded as part of your existence. Take a moment to consider how many actions you have performed already in your lifetime and how many thoughts you have had since birth until now. The number would be staggering – too staggering for your brain to compute. But every one of your thoughts and actions is recorded, which is where the Masonic symbol of the pencil comes into play.

The pencil symbolises the record of every thought and action you've ever performed and will ever perform. Thoughts and actions that, once made, can never be reversed. They are recorded as part of your life, written into eternity.

Where are your thoughts and actions recorded? In time? In space? In the log book of eternity? Perhaps they are recorded in something known as the Akashic records.

The Akashic records are believed to exist on the astral plane – that is, a non-physical plane– and is a compendium of all the universe's knowledge. It is said to contain a record of every thought and action of every person that ever existed. The name derives from the Sanskrit word 'akasha' which translates as 'space' or 'sky'. They are the records of all existence, from the beginning of time, logged for eternity.

The idea of an all-encompassing logbook of our thoughts and actions entered modern theosophical thinking through the writings of Helena Petrovna Blavatsky, the Russian philosopher and occultist, who talked of the 'indestructible tablets of astral light.'

The term 'Akashic records' first entered public spotlight through the writing of Alfred Percy Sinnett, an English author and theosophist, who in his 1884 book *Esoteric Buddhism* wrote of a 'permanency of the records in the Akasa' and a belief that humans could access these records.[86]

Fifteen years later, C. W. Leadbeater, a prolific author, member of the Theosophical Society, and a Freemason (he was initiated into Masonry in 1915), further popularised the existence of the Akashic records in his book *Clairvoyance.*

Alice Ann Bailey, a writer, philosopher, theosophist, and healer, wrote of the Akashic records in her book *Light of the Soul on The Yoga Sutras of Patanjali - Book 3 - Union achieved and its Results:* 'The Akashic record is like an immense photographic film, registering all the desires and earth experiences of our planet. Those who perceive it will see pictured thereon: The life experiences of every human being since time began, the reactions to experience of the entire animal kingdom, the aggregation of the thought-forms of a karmic nature (based on desire) of every human unit throughout time.'

The term 'Akashic records' may be a couple of centuries old but the idea of a compendium of all the knowledge of the universe is ancient. The Bible makes several mentions of a book in which all actions and knowledge are recorded:

Exodus. 32:33 'And the Lord said to Moses, "Whoever has sinned against Me, I will blot him out of My book."'

Psalms. 139:16 'Thine eyes did see my substance, yet being unperfect; and in thy book all my members were written, which in continuance were fashioned, when as yet there was none of them.'

Luke 10:20 '... but rejoice that your names are recorded in heaven.'

Revelations. 3:5 'He that overcometh, the same shall be clothed in white raiment; and I will not blot out his name out of the book of life, but I will confess his name before my Father, and before his angels.'

Revelations 17:8 '... and those who dwell on the earth will wonder, whose name has not been written in the book of life from the foundation of the world, when they see the beast, that he was and is not and will come.'

Revelations 20:12 'And I saw the dead, the great and the small, standing before the throne, and books were opened; and another book was opened, which is the book of life; and the dead were judged from the things which were written in the books, according to their deeds.'

Revelations 20:15 'And if anyone's name was not found written in the book of life, he was thrown into the lake of fire.'

Philippians 4:3 '...the rest of my fellow workers, whose names are in the book of life.'

Daniel 12:1 'And there will be a time of distress such as never occurred since there was a nation until that time; and at that time your people, everyone who is found written in the book, will be rescued.'

The Akashic records is believed to be a logbook of all souls, detailing their past lives, present lives and possible future existences. Sometimes called the 'zero point field', the Akashic field stores these records as energy. The zero point field is said to be the energy that is behind all other energy. It is described as a reservoir that holds all the energy from which everything manifests. More than just a record of the actions of every soul, the Akashic Records is also believed to be a compendium of humankind's collective wisdom.[87] Recent scientific discoveries prove the existence of the zero point field as a sea of fluctuating energies from which everything in the universe derives, including atoms, stars, planets, galaxies and even consciousness. This zero point field, or Akashic field, is the universe's memory and creation centre.[88]

What an amazing concept! The entire collection of human wisdom from the first man until now.

According to many clairvoyants and psychic healers, it is possible for any person to access the Akashic records, not only of their lives but the record of all human life and knowledge. American mystic, clairvoyant and healer, Edgar Cayce, known as the Sleeping Prophet, was able to put himself into a trance in which state he could access all the knowledge of the world and tap into the thoughts and knowledge of any person, alive or dead. He used this knowledge to predict future events and to heal those with whom he consulted.

Cayce wrote: 'Upon time and space is written the thoughts, the deeds, the activities of an entity – as in relationships to its environs, its hereditary influence; as directed – or judgment drawn by or according to what the entity's ideal is. Hence, as it has been oft called, the record is God's book of remembrance; and each entity, each soul – as the activities of a single day of an entity in the material world – either makes same good or bad or indifferent, depending upon the entity's application of self towards that which is the ideal manner for the use of time, opportunity and the expression of that for which each soul enters a material manifestation. The interpretation then as drawn here is with the desire and hope that, in opening this for the entity, the experience may be one of helpfulness and hopefulness.'

Cayce's ability to heal during these states of trance is legendary. He was able to diagnose and prescribe for someone who was with him in person during a trance, or someone who was a distance away, so long as he was provided with their name and location.

More amazing is the fact that Cayce was not a doctor but a simple man with a high school equivalent education. An example of Cayce's incredible ability is in the treatment of a developmentally disabled girl named Aimee Dietrich. Aimee suffered terrible seizures, untreatable by doctors. But after sessions with Cayce she returned to normal health.[90] Dietrich developed seizures when she was just two years old after an attack of La Grippe. She had her first reading with Cayce when she was five years old and he was twenty-five. After following the recommendations in Cayce's readings, Dietrich was seizure-free for about fourteen years.

Cayce made over 14,000 journeys to this plane of astral knowledge, which he also referred to as the Hall of Records. He described one of the journeys of his astral body to this Hall of Records as: 'Quite suddenly I come upon a Hall of Records. It is a hall without walls, without ceiling, but I am conscious of seeing an old man who hands me a large book, a record of the individual for whom I seek information.'[91]

With this knowledge of the Akashic records, the Book of Life, the Hall of Records, a universal super computer in which all our actions and thoughts are stored, the symbol of the Masonic pencil takes on a deep and important meaning. The prolific Masonic author, W. L. Wilmshurst, writes of the pencil in his book *The Meaning of Masonry:* 'He learns that old scores due by him to his fellowmen must be paid off and old wrongs righted, and receives the wages of past sins recorded upon his sub-consciousness by that pencil that observes, and there records, all our thoughts, words and actions.'[92]

By symbolic use of something as simple as a pencil, Masonry teaches that every thought, every action, every deed, is recorded in an eternal book. These thoughts and actions can never be erased. Once a thought occurs and an action performed, it is etched into eternity, in the Book of Life, the Akashic records, the astral plane's super computer, the universe's Google.

Whether or not you believe such a cosmic record exists, the lesson here is important. If your next action (the product of thought) is so poor that you would not dare post it on your Facebook status, don't perform such an action.

Even though we like to think we're alone with our thoughts, we are not. There is a higher power watching everything we do, tracking and recording our every thought and action. Call this higher power what you will: God, the Creator, Supreme Being, life force, eternal energy, or the universe. Know that it is watching you at all times. Hold yourself accountable for all of your thoughts and actions because once recorded they are never erased.

What we do is energy, and energy can't be destroyed. Next time you interact with someone, or perform a task, think about the symbolic pencil and ask yourself if your actions warrant being written into the Akashic record of your life.

In many ways a pencil is representative of your very self. Through thoughts and actions you are writing your life and leaving your impression on the pages of history.

Just as a pencil is sharpened the better to write with, so you have the means through education to acquire new skills and knowledge to sharpen yourself and better write your life story. A pencil on its own is an inanimate object. Once the pencil is taken in the hand of a higher power, it is capable through the assistance of that higher power to achieve great things.

Finally, and most importantly when regarding the pencil as a symbol of yourself, understand that it is what's inside the pencil that really matters. A pencil without lead, is just a hollow wooden shell.

The pencil is the only working tool in Freemasonry used operatively in the lodge room. Just as the Akashic records is a compendium of the thoughts, actions and wisdom of mankind, the secretary of a lodge, writing by hand (never by keyboard) is responsible for compiling the minutes of each meeting – the lodge's own Hall of Records – thus recording each and every thought and action of the lodge for eternity.

Life Application
Think before you act. If your actions are not worthy of posting on a Facebook status, do not perform such actions.

It is important to reflect on your actions each day and ask yourself whether such actions were worthy of inclusion into the universal record book of your life.

If someone reads a book of the actions you performed today, would they smile or would they cringe?

Make an effort in your next set of actions, particularly those involving interaction with someone else, to perform in such a way that is worthy of being written into the record of your life.

You cannot erase from your life actions already performed, but you can reflect on those actions, study their cause and effect, and ascertain the worthiness of those actions.

The past is permanent. History can't be changed but it can be used to teach you how to avoid repeating poor actions that may adversely affect your future.

Ask Yourself
- What was my first interaction with another person today?
- Were my actions worthy of entry into the universal record book of my life?
- What was the last action I performed that was not worthy of entry into the universal record book of my life?
- If someone was reading a book of my entire life, my every thought and action, would they smile or would they cringe?
- Can I make a conscious effort to treat the next person I meet in a way fit to be

written into the universal record book of my life?
- What actions from my life would I most like to erase if I could?
- What actions from my life would I not erase but would rewrite if I could?

From darkness
Light

Ignorance is the curse of God; knowledge is the wing wherewith we fly to heaven.
— William Shakespeare

While not as conspicuous as some of its better known counterparts, light is a symbol at the centre of Masonic teaching and may be the greatest of all symbols.

The word 'light' is referenced several times during the three Masonic degrees. When the candidate for Freemasonry is first presented to the Master of the lodge, he is asked of what he is in search. The candidate responds that he is in search of light in Masonry. In the second degree the candidate asks for 'more light in Masonry.' In the third and final degree, he asks for 'further light in Masonry.' This is, in fact, all the candidate ever asks of Freemasonry. Never once does a candidate ask for guidance, secrets, knowledge, direction or information. He only ever asks for light.

What exactly is the light the candidate seeks?

In the three degrees of Masonry the candidate is blindfolded when he enters the lodge room and forced to tread carefully as he tracks long circuits in a state of complete darkness. This process is an ancient initiation ritual called the Rite of Circumambulation, practiced by the Greeks, Romans, Hindus and Druids.

Shrouded in darkness as he performs a circumambulation of the lodge room, is it physical light the candidate seeks?

The answer is two-fold. Yes, the candidate does ask for physical light through the removal of the blindfold to restore his vision. Nevertheless, the transition from blindness to sight is symbolic of something far greater than the restoration of physical light.

It is said that the light of a Master Mason is darkness visible. Here we have the duality of light and dark represented by that other Masonic symbol of the checkered floorboard or mosaic pavement. There is no light without darkness, just as there is no chicken without an egg. Which came first, light or darkness? Unlike the 'chicken or the egg' debate, which can be argued both ways, the answer as to whether light or darkness came first is definitive: darkness.

The Mayans knew such when they said, 'Out of darkness comes light.' The beginning of the Old Testament tells us in Genesis 1:2: '... the earth was formless and empty; darkness was over the surface of the deep.'

Human life begins in the darkness of the womb. Daytime begins only when the sun rises, thus dispersing the darkness of night. Light cannot exist without darkness as the darkness of night is dissipated only by the rays of the morning sun. Where there is light, there is no darkness.

Primitive races considered darkness a cause of fear and, therefore, evil. They believed the magnificent sun, that sparkling great light, which climbed across the sky each day and gave rise to their crops – their lifeline – died when it dipped below the horizon, killed off by the darkness of night.

At night, the underworld took possession of the sun. Through a display of enormous strength – *Sol Invictus* – the sun overcame the adversity of evil and rose triumphantly from the dead the following morning. When the sun reappeared over the Eastern horizon and the last bits of darkness (evil) were vanquished from the sky, order was restored. The good of the sun, as always, overcame death and kicked night's evil butt.

Sunlight was a symbol of life for primitive man. He realised that when the sun was in the sky and he basked in its light, he felt happier than he did at night. He didn't know about solar energy, the synthesis of Vitamin D, photosensitivity or melatonin. The sun made the plants grow, allowed his children to play outside, brought the animals to life, allowed him to hunt with full vision, gave warmth against the cold, and felt good on his skin. The sun and thus light, therefore, was a source of goodness.

Nature gives you all you need for a healthy existence, two of the necessities for which are water and sunlight. Without either, you cannot survive. Sunlight improves your mood by boosting levels of serotonin, the body's natural happy hormone, and increases the release of endorphins, especially through outdoor exercise. An increase in serotonin also helps suppress the appetite, aiding in weight loss, and is the reason we tend to eat less during the summer than in the winter.

Exposure to sunlight during the day increases melatonin, which helps to regulate sleep at night. This is why the body requires less sleep during summer, and why we feel more alive in the summer than in the winter when the sun is not as strong. Sunlight allows the skin to synthesise Vitamin D, which promotes calcium absorption in the intestines and helps the development of strong bones. Sunlight improves the functioning of the liver and the kidneys. Sweat created by sunlight helps eliminate waste from the body.

As with everything in life, sunlight is a duality. Incorrect exposure to sunlight can cause harm. Too much exposure to sunlight on your skin may result in cancer. Knowing how much sunlight to absorb into your body is the key to reaping its benefits. As you will soon see, knowledge – light – is often a double-edged sword.

In various forms of meditation, practitioners visualise being surrounded by white light. Modern healers believe that the envisioning of white light contributes to spiritual healing and, using the adage of 'as above, so below', this white spiritual light positively affects the physical self. Light meditation, also known as the 'white-light method', is used to achieve a state of peace through the enhancement of personal energy. It is accomplished by visualising every breath as an intake of white light and every exhale as the pushing out of black smoke, symbolic of negative energy leaving the body. The practitioner then visualises a beam of intense white light entering into the body through the top of the head, proceeding down the entire body, then back up through the spine. The energy of the whiteness visualised is said to induce a state of joy in which negative energy is dispelled from the body.

I am not endorsing the practice of white light meditation. However if such a form of meditation empowers you and allows you to feel a sense of peace, joy, harmony, and protection, then by all means give it a go. I've heard stories of people being chased by a mugger and envisioning a white light about them, which made them invisible to the mugger. Are such stories true? I'm not one to discredit someone else's experience. After all, the acquisition of knowledge is a system of experience. What works for some, may not work for others. The point being that light is a powerful force if you choose to empower it, be it physical light or spiritual light.

All ancient systems revered light as a representation of good over the darkness of evil, of two antagonistic principles. Pythagoras considered light a symbol of unity, equality, and stability; darkness a symbol of inequality and instability. To the colour white, which is only seen with light, he attached goodness; to the colour black, which is the result of an absence of light, he attached evil.

Gerald Massey (1828-1907), an English poet and author on spiritualism and Ancient Egypt, wrote of the symbolism of light and darkness: 'The Hebrew devil, or Satan, means the opponent or adversary, and the first great natural adversary recognised by primitive man was Darkness – simply darkness, the constant and eternal enemy of the light – that is, the power of darkness was literal before it became metaphorical, moral, or spiritual.

'Hence darkness itself was the earliest devil or adversary, the obstructor and deluder of man, the eternal enemy of the sun. We speak of the 'jaws of darkness'; and darkness was the vast, huge, swallower of the light, night after night. We know this was identified as the primary power, because the primitive or early man reckoned time by nights, and the years by eclipses. This mode of reckoning was first and universal. So many darks preceded so many days. The dark power is primarily in all the oldest traditions and cults of the human race. Hence, sacrifice was first offered to the powers of darkness. The forewords of universal mythology are 'there was darkness'. All was dark at first within the mind; and the *all* was the *darkness* that created dread without. The influence of night, the eclipse, and the black thundercloud being first felt, the primitive man visibly emerges from the shadow of darkness as deeply impressed and indelibly dyed in mind, as was his body with its natural blackness. The black man without was negroid within, as his reflection remains in the mirror of mythology. The darkness then, in natural phenomena, was the original devil that put out the light by swallowing it incessantly, as the subtle enemy, the obstructor, deluder, and general adversary of man.'[93]

It is easy to see how light and darkness transformed from the physical to the symbolic, and why goodness was attached to one, and evil to the other. Even today, darkness is considered the abode of evil. Small children are afraid of the dark but not of the light. Adults use the term, 'I wouldn't want to meet him in a dark alley' when discussing someone possessing a hurtful or evil nature.

Darkness itself is not evil, of course. A great many good things happen in darkness. We, however, are creatures of light, and require light to see and comprehend objects. Take away the light and fear develops. Darkness impairs our senses, affects our brains, and puts us in dangerous situations.

Let's use the example of driving down a country highway. You're driving through a pitch black night lit in part only by your car's headlights. If you turn off the headlights you're suddenly driving in complete darkness, unable to see the twists and turns in the road. The darkness will not kill you – your inability to follow the road due to a lack of light is what will cause an accident. Without the use of headlights, you have no knowledge of what lies ahead. You're driving blind. Turning on your headlights puts you back in control. The headlights illuminate the path ahead, giving you knowledge of the upcoming twists and turns, thus creating safety.

There is no evil in darkness; there is only the perception of evil. Remember, evil is part of the duality of existence. It is part of the other side of nature. It is the winter to the summer, the night to the day, the storm to the clear skies. The other sides of the positives of life are not to be feared, they are to be understood.

Light is knowledge, and knowledge is a pathway. We can only walk along a path we see; otherwise, we are stumbling about and stubbing our toes against the bed-corners of life.

Sometimes light doesn't simply guide us down a path, it pulls us. It's not surprising that people who have had near death experiences (NDE's) describe being pulled toward a great, powerful and brilliant light. The 'tunnel experience' of most NDE's involves being drawn through a dark tunnel until reaching a realm of radiant golden-white light. Once in the light, NDE's describe being engulfed in great light in which they receive an overwhelming feeling of peace, joy and harmony. There they interact with deceased friends or relatives who glow with inner light and radiate pure love. NDE's commonly report a sense of greater consciousness during their experience, and a sense of greater understanding of all things and how the universe fits together.

Edgar Cayce, the American mystic, clairvoyant, and healer, wrote extensively of his out of body experiences while in a trance-like state where, it is said, he could access all the knowledge of the universe. He wrote;

'I see myself as a tiny dot out of my physical body, which lies inert before me. I find myself oppressed by darkness and there is a feeling of terrific loneliness. Suddenly, I am conscious of a white beam of light, knowing that I must follow it or be lost. As I move along this path of light I gradually become conscious of various levels upon which there is movement. Upon the first levels there are vague, horrible shapes, grotesque forms such as one sees in nightmares. Passing on, there begins to appear on either side misshapen forms of human beings with some part of the body magnified. Again there is change, and I become conscious of grey-hooded forms moving downward. Gradually, these become lighter in colour. Then the direction changes and these forms move upward and the colour of the robes grows rapidly lighter. Next, there begins to appear on either side vague outlines of houses, walls, trees, etc., but everything is motionless. As I pass on, there is more light and movement in what appear to be normal cities and towns. With the growth of movement I become conscious of sounds, at first indistinct rumblings, then music, laughter, and singing of birds. There is more and more light, the colours become very beautiful, and there is the sound of wonderful music.'[94]

To go into the light is to be lead to heaven. Heaven is not a physical place beyond death of the body, but a state of higher existence, above and beyond the physical state we are confined to while in Earthly form. It is a state in which all knowledge – all light – is revealed. It is a state in which the pure energy of the soul has none of the limitations it was forced to act within while residing in physical form. In heaven, the soul is no longer hindered from its full expression.

It is not uncommon for people who have had a near death experience to describe such a state. Take, for example, the comments of Michael F., an NDE from the website nderf.org (Near Death Experience Research Foundation):

'I found myself immersed in this all-encompassing light where time has no meaning. Space has no meaning. I have a feeling of oneness with the Universe. The pull of this light is so captivating and overwhelming that I have no choice but to completely surrender to it. It reminded me of shimmering liquid mercury. My natural instincts tell me to look left and right. I manage to look two degrees in both directions before I am instantly drawn back to the centre. The attraction I feel towards this light fills me with total awe. The unconditional love, peace and happiness it exudes are infinite'.[95]

Sounds like heaven, doesn't it? Let's bring the symbol of light back down to Earth.

In a Masonic lodge, the candidate is lead around the lodge room in a circuit following the path of the sun. He is inspected by the three principles officers of the lodge: the Master in the East representing the rising sun; the Junior Warden in the South representing the sun at its meridian; and the Senior Warden in the West representing the setting sun. The candidate is never received in the North. Why? Traditionally the North is a place of darkness. As Albert Mackey tells us in his *Encyclopedia of Freemasonry*: 'The sun in his progress through the ecliptic never reaches farther than 23° 28' north of the equator. A wall being erected on any part of the earth farther north than that, will therefore, at meridian, receive the rays of the sun only on its south side, while the north will be entirely in shadow at the hour of meridian.'

The organisation of officers along the path of the sun is not unique to Freemasonry. In the mystery schools of India, the chief officers were positioned in the East, West and South as Brahma, Vishnu and Shiva to represent the rising, meridian, and setting sun. The chief officer of the Druids sat in the East assisted by two officers who sat in the West and the South, representing the moon and the midday sun. These three positions have always represented the threefold division of power and completeness: Father, Son, Holy Spirit; mind, body, soul; past, present, future; religion, science, art. Add to these the sum of human capability as thought, word and deed. Three kinds of matter: animal, vegetable, and mineral. Three attributes of God: omniscience, omnipresence, and omnipotence. And the three virtues of Masonry: faith, hope, and charity.

The sun is known as one of the three lesser lights of Masonry, the other two being the moon and the Master of the lodge. It is the Master's job to manage the lodge with the same equal regularity as the sun manages the day and the moon manages the night.

As master in control of your own personal lodge you should regulate your entire being as the sun regulates your physicality. This self-regulation requires finding a balance between your sun and moon – between your conscious and subconscious, your masculine and feminine – to become the true master of your self. The sun represents your masculine nature and the moon your feminine side. Only through balance of this duality can you master yourself, completing a triangle equal in all its sides, which is the representation of perfection.

The candidate in Masonry is always kept in the sunlight, which is representative of always soaking in the rays of knowledge. So long as the candidate stays in the symbolic light of the Sun – goodness, knowledge, and higher learning – he will not err.

Upon removal of the blindfold, the candidate is brought from darkness to light. Indeed the first objects the candidate sees after the removal of the blindfold are the Three Great Lights in Masonry, which are the Volume of the Sacred Law (the book of one's faith),square and compasses. These three Great Lights hold the key to new knowledge. Like a newborn baby, the candidate sees everything (symbolically) for the first time and, like a child, is ready to absorb new knowledge that will elevate him above the darkness of his purely physical self. He is ready to be enlightened.

All natural light comes from the Sun and stars. Light travels at a speed of 186,000 miles a second and takes 8 minutes and 17 seconds to travel from the Sun's surface to Earth. Light starts with atoms, which are a nucleus surrounded by electrons that orbit. Just like the solar system, these electrons remain in orbit unless the electrons get kicked into a different orbit, which is done by adding energy to an atom through heat. When the atom cools, the electrons return to their original orbit and in doing so emit light. Each electron returning to its orbit emits one photon of light. The colour of this light is determined by how big the electron's jump is between orbits. When you combine all the colours together, you get white light. It is white light that enables us to see.

White light is known also as 'visible light', which is kind of misleading. White light allows us to see, but within white light is contained every imaginable colour, all of which our human eyes cannot perceive. This is another reason why light is symbolic of knowledge. Knowledge is learning, and learning is the acquisition of facts, information, skills, truths, principles and awareness. Newly acquired information is said to 'come to light', which means such knowledge is brought out of darkness. This information was never secret, it was just hidden under the veil of darkness until coming to light, which is darkness made visible. Darkness represents ignorance. Light represents knowledge. Ignorance is the enemy of knowledge. All the knowledge of the world is available to us once we shed our ignorance.

That's nonsense! you may be thinking. *I can't possibly learn ALL the knowledge of the world. It would take ten lifetimes if not more!*

Nobody said you need to learn all the knowledge of the world. You need acquire only that knowledge pertinent to your own existence. What knowledge you let enter your life is entirely your choice. You can choose to embrace the knowledge of how to live a better life (embrace the light) or you can choose to ignore such knowledge (reside in darkness). The choice is yours.

Symbolic light appears several times throughout the Old and New Testaments of the Bible. In Matthew 6:22, Jesus says: 'The eye is the lamp of the body; so then if your eye is clear, your whole body will be full of light'.

The eyes are said to be the window to the soul. What is the purpose of a window? To let in light. Ninety-eight percent of light enters the body through the eyes. The best source of light is sunlight, which is another reason why the Sun was venerated by ancient cultures and still plays a central role in Masonry today.

The soul is nourished by both physical light and the light of knowledge. If your soul is clear, which is achieved through living an upright and loving life, your whole character will be clear. If your soul is polluted by evildoings or a life succumbed to base/animal instincts and materialism, your soul will be defiled and your character tarnished. Good brings about good; bad brings about bad. Stay in the light, which is where good resides.

Light allows us to see vision as a matter of perception. What one sees as right, another sees as wrong. It is important for you to see things in the right light; otherwise, you may commit wrongdoings yet think you're acting rightly.

Like everything in life, there is a duality to knowledge. The trick to successfully attaining knowledge is to understand its application for the betterment of your life, not for its detriment. For example, primitive man's discovery of fire and its creation provided the means to generate warmth and cook food (good knowledge), but also developed into a means to create unprecedented devastation through human hands (knowledge used detrimentally). The technology used to fly a plane and allow people to travel and experience the world is the same technology used to fly a missile capable of destroying lives. The Chinese were looking to develop a potion for immortality when they invented gunpowder. Originally, they used gunpowder to make fireworks to scare away evil spirits, and later weaponised their creation for destructive purposes – ironically, the exact opposite of the immortality they'd first hoped to achieve.

We read in Matthew 6:24 that, 'no one can serve two masters.' A man cannot devote his time and attention solely to the material comforts of life and greater prosperity, lest he become a slave to the material. While we live in a material world, we must pay attention to the material but not let it dictate our character. The only true way to master ourselves is by transcending our animal instincts. They key to a good life is to achieve balance between the material and the spiritual, the meeting of the horizontal (material) and the perpendicular (spiritual), the result of which is the formation of a right angle, as discussed previously. How to achieve this balance requires knowledge, which is symbolised by light.

Light is a central symbol of Freemasonry. In fact, it may be viewed as *the* essential symbol of Freemasonry as without light, all is darkness. An illumination from the metaphorical darkness of ignorance is what the true Freemason seeks.

A newly raised Master Mason is told he has received all the light that can be conferred in a lodge of Master Masons. This is only partially true. The new Master Mason has received all the light (knowledge) that exists in the words and actions of the Masonic ritual; however his search for further light (more knowledge) is never ending.

When a Karate practitioner receives a black belt, his learning does not end, rather he is told that true learning is just beginning. As a black belt he now has all the tools necessary to pursue harder physical techniques, as well as the internal aspects of the martial arts. Sure, he has mastered the art of punching and kicking to black belt level, but has he mastered his thoughts, his breathing, his character?

Knowledge is a lifelong pursuit. Just when you think you know it all, you realise that you really don't know anything. There's a whole world of knowledge out there waiting to be accessed, absorbed, and used to improve all aspects of life: physical, psychical, and spiritual.

The light of knowledge is not knowledge for knowledge's sake. A man with an office wall full of diplomas and certificates is not necessarily more enlightened than the janitor who cleans the man's office at night. Book Smart vs Street Smart is a topic of much debate. Some will argue that you don't need a college degree to be successful. After all, Steve Jobs and Steve Wozniak, co-founders of Apple, did not have college degrees. The same goes for Bill Gates and Richard Branson. However, in the United States the unemployment rate for people without a high school diploma is significantly larger than for those with a bachelor's degree.

Those who learn via analytical intelligence (book smart) are able to process transmitted knowledge effectively and comprehend more complex concepts. Those who learn through practical knowledge (street smart) learn most effectively through their own experiences and are able to use these experiences to adapt to new experiences.

Which is a better way to acquire knowledge? It doesn't matter. What matters is that the knowledge acquired illuminates your life and elevates your existence. Perhaps a better word for it is wisdom.

The dictionary defines wisdom as: *the quality or state of being wise; knowledge of what is true or right coupled with just judgment as to action; sagacity, discernment, or insight.*

Wisdom has been long deemed one of the most important qualities a person can possess. 'Wisdom, compassion, and courage are the three universally recognised moral qualities of men,' said Confucius. Any man can be smart, but few men are wise. There's a big difference between the two.

Socrates said, 'Wisdom begins in wonder.' While Buddha said, 'Just as treasures are uncovered from the earth, so virtue appears from good deeds, and wisdom appears from a pure and peaceful mind. To walk safely through the maze of human life, one needs the light of wisdom and the guidance of virtue.'

In Taoism it is said, 'Knowing others is intelligence; knowing yourself is true wisdom. Mastering others is strength; mastering yourself is true power.' In Hinduism, wisdom is considered a state of mind through which is the soul achieves freedom. To be wise is to know yourself and to live rightly.

Knowledge of yourself comes with balance. You must know how to live in balance with the light and dark dualities of life. The same thing that gives you power can also kill you. This is the nature of the world. A daffodil needs sunlight to survive. Too much sunlight and it will die; too little sunlight and it will also die. The key to the daffodil's survival is finding balance between too much and too little. The same applies to you. If your skin experiences too much sunlight, you may die. If your skin experiences too little sunlight, you may die. Everything in life is about balance.

Light overcomes darkness, as knowledge overcomes fear, and true knowledge is wisdom. Darkness is one of the most basic primal fears that a person first experiences as a child. It is only when the knowledge that the darkness itself can't hurt us – our mother telling us in the comfort of her cradling arms that there's nothing to be scared of – that our fear is overcome. What we thought was scary was not, and we no longer have fear. We recognise fear for what it is: **F**alse **E**vidence **A**ppearing **R**eal.

Through real (**R**ight **E**vidence **A**ttaining **L**ight) knowledge and the acquisition of true wisdom, the falsities of life are dispelled. Once light overcomes darkness – the darkness of our own character and the dark corners of our psyche formed by our natural attraction to our animal instincts – we bring our life into balance and harmony.

The light of Freemasonry is threefold in its meaning. It symbolises:

* the importance of physical light necessary for the optimum functioning of the human body;
*the constant acquisition of knowledge by which wisdom is derived;
*the light of your true self, your divine spark, the most beautiful part of who you are.

The third aspect of this triple symbolism is a call to let your real self shine and never to shy away from light. As much as you need let light shine on you, it is essential to let your inner light shine outward.

Light is both received and given; absorbed and dispersed; internal and external. Let your light shine on others to enable them to emerge from their own darkness and in turn shine their inner light.

Light is always in motion and never still. Like light, you must always be in motion, aspiring to greater heights. Never become stagnant. Keep chasing the metaphoric Sun or you will be left standing, idle and useless, in darkness.

Life Application

Is your life shrouded in darkness or bathed in light?

Are you constantly increasing your knowledge and allowing light to pour into your psychical and spiritual self?

Life is full of dualities. You have the choice of either walking in darkness, remaining ignorant to elevating yourself above your animal nature, or walking in the symbolic light of constant self-improvement.

Before undertaking any action, particularly actions toward another person, ask yourself: will this action be bathed in light or shrouded in darkness?

What parts of your life are problematic right now?

Finances?

Relationships?

Health?

Try to discover the root of the cause in your problems, then work on 'shedding light' on these problems. Sometimes problems exist and persist because we are not willing to acknowledge them, that is, we are not willing to 'bring them to light.' It is only when light is shed on any situation that it becomes truly visible and a remedy applied.

Empower your life by increasing knowledge, in particular the knowledge that is pertinent to yourself and your surroundings. By increasing knowledge you will increase wisdom, which is one of the most important traits a person can possess.

Knowledge is 'power of the mind', and wisdom is the power of the mind to apply your knowledge at the right moment at the appropriate place and situation. Acting with wisdom brings us in harmony with ourselves, giving us a sense of self-worth and inner peace. This inner peace is achieved because we are acting in accordance with our conscience and avoiding the shame and guilt of following our baser instincts.

Ask Yourself
- What aspects of my life are shrouded in darkness and how can I shed light upon them?

- Did my actions today follow the path of my symbolic sun? Did I shed light on myself or stand in the darkness of ignorance?
- What is a problem currently affecting my life? What part of this problem lies in symbolic darkness, and what part of it is in symbolic light?
- Did I act in light or darkness in my interactions with people today?
- Did I advance my personal knowledge today?
- Sunlight is important to my health. Am I getting enough?
- Do the people in my life radiate light or do I reflect their darkness?
- Am I preventing someone else from shining? Do I cast darkness over others?

To see or not to see
The All-Seeing Eye

It is a terrible thing to see and have no vision.

— Helen Keller

The All-Seeing Eye is one of the most debated symbols in Freemasonry. Trumped up by conspiracy theorists as an allusion to big brother government watching our every move, the All-Seeing Eye is a simple and meaningful symbol that teaches a comforting lesson.

The Masonic All-Seeing Eye is rooted in antiquity and can be traced back to Ancient Egypt and the symbol of the Eye of Horus, who was the national patron god of Egypt. Also known as the Eye of Providence, the All-Seeing Eye is found throughout the world from Egyptian hieroglyphs to the Mormon Temple in Salt Lake City, the Kazan Cathedral and Alexander Column in St. Petersburg, Russia,[96] the Aachen Cathedral in Germany[97], and various churches throughout the United States, Argentina, South Africa and beyond. The eye is sometimes depicted behind a veil, within a triangle or radiating beams of light.

At its most basic, the All-Seeing Eye is a symbol of omniscience, from the Latin *omnis* meaning 'all' and *sciens* meaning 'knowing' (from which derives the English word 'science'). The All-Seeing Eye symbolises an omniscient deity, a divine being or a higher power that knows all and sees all. This higher power keeps a watchful eye on all things, especially the actions of man.

Freemasonry teaches that the All-Seeing Eye looks into the inner most recesses of the heart and rewards the individual according to the works of his heart.

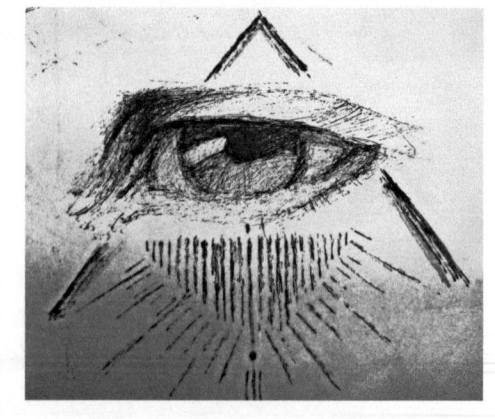

In this sense, the All-Seeing Eye corresponds closely in symbolism to that of the pencil, as discussed in a previous chapter. A symbol of the Third Degree of Masonry, the pencil symbolises the record of every thought and action that once made, can never be reversed. Each action and thought is recorded as part of your life, written into eternity. By symbolic use of the pencil, Masonry teaches that every thought, every action, every deed, is recorded in an eternal book. Once a thought is experienced and an action performed, it is etched into eternity, in the Book of Life, the Akashic Records, the zero point field. Similarly, the All-Seeing Eye teaches of a higher power watching over everything we do, and from whose gaze nothing is hidden. All our actions are held accountable by the universe. Everything we do must conform to the Universal Law.

What is the Universal Law?

The Universal Laws, also referred to as Spiritual Laws or the Laws Of Nature, are the unwavering and unchanging principles that govern every aspect of the universe, and are the means by which our world and the entire cosmos continues to exist, thrive and expand.

The Universal Law is the law that binds us all. The universe exists by virtue of the Universal Law, which forms its framework and holds it together. Every cause has its effect; every effect has its cause; everything happens according to law. Good and bad actions produce their respective pleasant and painful effects regardless of the ideology and aspirations of those who engage in them. This is the basis of the Universal Law, at the heart of which is the adage: *Do unto others as you would have them do unto you.*

The prime Universal Law states all beings are sovereign and have free will to express their creative urges in any way they choose, but no being has the right to violate and harm others. All beings, guided by the Universal Law, are prohibited from performing actions that would harm others. We should respect the rights and boundaries of one another. This is also known as the Golden Rule.

For as long as men have instructed in ethics, the ethic of reciprocity has existed. Confucius said: 'Never impose on others what you would not choose for yourself.' Plato wrote in his dialogue *Crito*: 'One should never do wrong in return, nor mistreat any man, no matter how one has been mistreated by him.' In addition, when Hilel was asked for a summary of the teachings of the entire Torah, he answered: 'That which is hateful to you, do not do to your fellow. That is the whole Torah; the rest is the explanation; go and learn it.'[98]

The All-Seeing Eye symbolises the watchfulness of a higher power. What's the point of such a symbol? The simple answer is conscience.

Though we should treat others as we wish to be treated, the Golden Rule doesn't always gel with our human nature. Sometimes we do bad stuff because, well, we think we can get away with it.

Take, for example, a simple excursion to the supermarket. You have a trolley full of goods and you proceed to the self-checkout where you swipe your purchases: apples, toilet paper, mustard, soft drink, chicken thighs, steaks…then you realise you can probably get away with not swiping the next item and you slip it in your bag. You swipe a couple of more items and then realise you can probably get away with not swiping something else, so you slip it into your bag. You pay for all your goods and exit the store, chuffed that you didn't pay for three or four items. You saved thirty pounds.

Realistically, however, you didn't *save* thirty pounds, you *stole* thirty pounds' worth of goods. You stole from the store, you stole from the supplier and even worse, you stole from the hard-working staff – the cashiers, the shelf-stockers, the produce-handlers – all of whom receive the average wage. You did all this to save a few quid. You did something to someone else that you would not want done to yourself. You defied Universal Law.

Why did you defy Universal Law? Because you knew you'd get away with it. You saw a shortcut and took it without consideration for those from whom you stole. Somebody has to account for the product you didn't pay for but hey, as long as you're up thirty pounds, who cares, right?

If you had checked out at the regular cashier, you would never have got away with stealing thirty pounds' worth of produce. The cashier would have kept an eye on everything in your trolley, making sure nothing was taken without payment. The cashier, in effect, would have been an All-Seeing Eye to your purchases.

The All-Seeing Eye is the universe's cashier and its CCTV. It's the referee who warns you *before* you commit a foul. It is the omniscience of a higher power watching all you do; it is your conscience, the little voice in your head, the angel on your shoulder that tells you not to succumb to your base instincts, to your crude nature, your animal self. It is the eye in the sky, watching, monitoring, and saying, 'Hey! Don't steal that produce! That's not the right thing to do.'

This is one of two symbolisms of the All-Seeing Eye. The other symbolism refers to what Buddhists call the 'Eye of Wisdom'.

It is a Buddhist belief that human beings have two kinds of eyes. One eye is the 'Worldly Eye' that sees material objects. This is our regular sight through which we see the world. The other eye is the Eye of Wisdom that sees our spiritual nature. Here, once again, we have the merging of our material self with our spiritual self, as discussed in previous chapters. It is the meeting of the horizontal/level (material) and perpendicular/plumb (spiritual) at a ninety-degree angle, forming a square. It is perfect balance.

When we see clearly through both eyes, we see our material and our spiritual sides as one and achieve clear vision. If we only look with our material eye, all we see are objects. If all we see are objects, we will act only on our crude/animal nature because a world of purely material objects leads to greed and ignorance, as in the example of stealing produce from the supermarket.

If we see only through our Eye of Wisdom, we will not be able to live in the material world in which we must exist. The key to living an upright life and being square in our actions is finding balance between the two.

Looking through two eyes – the Worldly Eye and the Eye of Wisdom – gives a clear vision of the world. This clear vision forms one picture, which is why the All-Seeing Eye is symbolised by a single eye rather than two eyes.

When we look at an object our brain turns the vision of two eyes into one sight, that is, we don't get two different perspectives of an object. The two become one, therefore in total we have three (2+1). The three is representative of our Third Eye. This Third Eye represents total awareness of the world around you, that is material and spiritual awareness. Ancient belief has it that a physical Third Eye exists in the pineal gland.

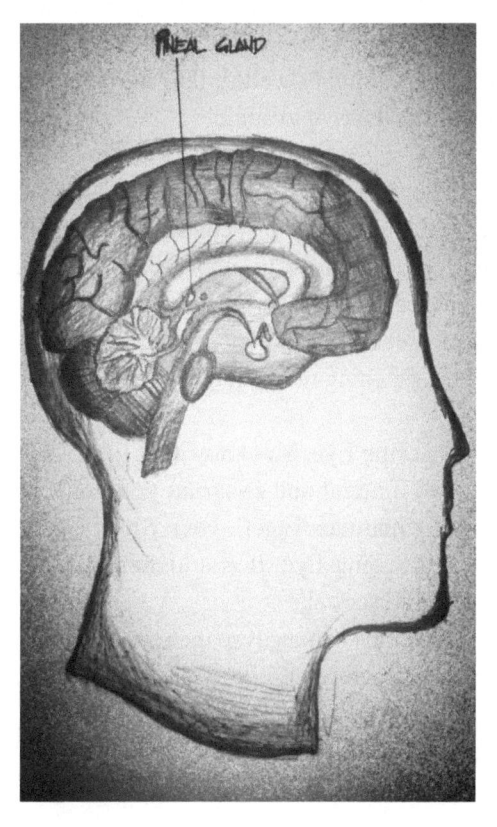

The pineal gland is located near the centre of the brain between the left and the right hemispheres (cerebral hemispheres). It is about the size of a pea and shaped like a pine cone, hence its name and the reason the pine cone was often used as a symbol of higher intelligence recognised by various ancient cultures as found in the ruins of the Indonesians, Babylonians, Egyptians, Greeks, Romans, and Christians.[99] The pine cone still finds prevalence in religion today. The Pope's staff features a carving of a pine cone and a visit to the Vatican will lead you to the Courtyard of the Pine, in which stands a bronze sculpture of a pine cone, more than 13 feet tall, flanked by two peacocks. Pine cones have long represented immortality, derived as they are from evergreen trees, and the spiral pattern of a pine cone reflects the

Fibonacci sequence in nature, the spiralling appearance of which is detailed in a previous chapter on the symbolism of the Winding Staircase.

Rene Descartes, the sixteenth century French philosopher, regarded the pineal gland as the principal seat of the soul and the place in which all our thoughts are formed.[100]

In Hindi tradition a small round dot called a bindi is placed on the forehead between the eyes, marking the Third Eye. It alludes to the location of the sixth chakra — 'Anja' — that deals with telepathy, imagination, visualisation and intuition, all of which contribute to clearer vision of one's spiritual nature over the material.[101] It is said that the sixth chakra is where a person's ego, habits, false ideas of racialism, and misidentifications are dissolved, which corresponds to the purpose of Freemasonry to subdue the passions. It is through this subduing of passions and learning to 'circumscribe our desires and keep our passions in due bounds' that we are able to elevate our consciousness and rise above our purely material selves.

The All-Seeing Eye of Freemasonry, therefore, is a symbol doubled with significance. First, it represents being watched over by a higher power that monitors your every action and guides you to do good through your conscience. Second, it is a call to balance your material vision with your spiritual vision, which is done through acquiring symbolic light (knowledge) and physical light (health), thus unifying in a third eye that represents the higher self you should strive to attain.

Life Application

Is something playing on your conscience? If the answer is yes, chances are you did something you didn't want the All-Seeing Eye to witness. In other words, you did something you shouldn't have done that opposed Universal Law.

Before you perform any action, visualise a security camera watching your every move. Now ask yourself: knowing a camera is watching me right now, will I perform the action of my thought?

You probably already use a symbolic All Seeing Eye. You know that little angel on your shoulder reprimanding you for a bad thought and ensuring you don't do anything silly or illegal? You may call it your 'Guardian Angel', your 'Spirit Guide' or 'someone watching over me'. It is the All-Seeing Eye. It is a higher power, a connection to the spiritual realm. It knows all and sees all.

Keep a written or a mental record of your actions and analyse them at day's end. Ask if your actions were performed by way of seeing through your Worldly Eye, through your Eye of Wisdom, or through a balance of both.

Ask Yourself
- Are any of my actions playing on my conscience?
- How can I clear my conscience?
- Do I have a thought in mind of performing an action that will go against my conscience?
- Did I do something today that, if someone was watching me, I wouldn't have done?
- Would I knowingly perform my next action if I knew someone was watching me?
- Am I allowing enough physical light into my body?
- Do any of the ailments I am currently experience come from a lack of physical light entering my body?
- How can I allow more sunlight into my body?
- Did I illuminate my mind today? Did I learn something new?
- What areas of my life lack illumination?
- What area of increased knowledge can I pursue to better my life?
- Is there a situation currently hampering my life? Is my perception of this situation evenly balanced between my Worldly Eye and my Eye of Wisdom?

No bones about it
The skull & crossbones

While I thought that I was learning how to live, I have been learning how to die.
— Leonardo Da Vinci

Associated with poison, pirates, and a college-based secret society that bears its name, the skull and crossbones is one of the most discussed and misunderstood of all symbols, and is never actually mentioned in any of the Masonic degrees.

If the skull and crossbones are never mentioned in any degree, how is it a Masonic symbol?

The answer lies in the tracing board[102] of the Master Mason degree, which depicts (among numerous other symbols) the skull and crossbones on a coffin. It should also be noted that the Order of the Temple Degree of York Rite Masonry (Knights Templar) uses prolific symbolism of the skull but not the crossbones.

In some lodges, such as the Australian lodge where I was made a Mason, a human skeleton is shown to the brother during the third degree ritual as a reminder that death is always near and could come at any time or place, regardless of a man's wealth, power or social status. Death, Masons are taught, is the great leveller and regards no man for his worldly possessions. In the ritual of the third degree, the candidate is taught that after acquiring knowledge and truth in life, he must next learn how to die. Masons are taught that after the mind is modelled by virtue and science, nature presents one final lesson for us all – to prepare for the last hours of our earthly existence.

This may sound grizzly by some interpretations. After all, who or what can teach you how to die? The concept of teaching someone how to die is, well, morbid. But another, truer interpretation is that we should never stop learning. Knowledge is illumination. Illumination makes the darkness disappear. That the third degree of Freemasonry teaches one how to die, doesn't mean it's a lesson on how to kill yourself.

Freemasonry teaches you to die with the knowledge that you did all you could to live a life modelled by virtue. Death, it is taught, is not as bad as the stain one brings to his symbolic apron by living a life of falsehood and dishonour. A just and virtuous man will reflect on the 'awful' subject of death.

Be careful here not to misinterpret the word 'awful' as something terrible, disagreeable or objectionable. Here the word 'awful' is defined as: *1. Inspiring awe; 2. Filled with awe.* Death is an awe-inspiring subject and to be prepared for it is to have a life of no regrets, a life of just and virtuous thoughts and actions. This, teaches Masonry, is how one prepares to die.

The association of the skull and crossbones with death has given an important symbol a bad rap. Indeed many a Mason is hesitant to discuss the meaning of the skull and crossbones beyond being a symbol of their own mortality. This hesitance, however, arises from a lack of knowledge as to the symbol's true meaning which, when learned, is strikingly beautiful. Believe it or not, the skull and crossbones is a symbol of life, not death.

The skull and crossbones also gets a bad rap due to its application as a modern symbol for poison and its proliferation in the mythology of seafaring pirates. Pirate captains of the eighteenth century used a black flag bearing skull and crossbones or, alternatively, a skull and crossed swords, known as a Jolly Roger. Many sports teams utilise the Jolly Roger or its variations as their club emblem, among them the Pittsburgh Pirates Major League Baseball team, and the Tampa Bay Buccaneers and Oakland Raiders American football teams.

As a Masonic symbol the skull and crossbones has nothing to do with pirates and poisons. It is neither morbid nor evil. Its true lesson is profound, to say the least.

In analysing the skull and crossbones symbol, it is necessary to break it down into its two parts: the skull and then the crossbones. Let's begin with the skull.

The skull, as you know, is the head's skeleton. It supports the structure of the face and provides a protective cavity for the brain. The skull allows the senses to operate effectively, particularly sight and sound. The fixed distance between the eyes, created by the skull, allows depth of perception of three-dimensional objects. In other words, though we see with two eyes, which is called binocular vision, we interpret objects with stereoscopic vision, which is the single perception of a slightly different image from each eye, providing a three dimensional view. The skull also fixes the position of the ears to allow us to hear properly with direction and distance. Without a skull, these senses would be impossible.

The skull's most important job is to protect the brain, without which we would not only be deprived of all senses, but of life itself. This makes the skull the most valuable set of bones in the body. The brain is surrounded by eight bones: one frontal bone; two parietal bones, two temporal bones, one occipital bone, one sphenoid bone and one ethmoid bone. These eight bones comprise the cranium. The rest of the skull comprises fourteen bones in the face and three small bones in each ear.

The place where the bones meet is called a suture. Sutures are flexible in children but become fixed with age. Symbolically, this aspect of the skull may represent the wonder with which we perceive the world as children and the stubborn, adamant adherence to our institutional programming we exhibit as adults in which our polarisation leaves no wiggle room. As we age, childhood wonderment is replaced by established conditioning, or reactive thought patterns, whereby our living reality is formed by repetitive societal, national, peer, family and religious dialogue to which the higher self becomes lowered, and the light of your divine spark more greatly dimmed by the ego. It is wise to often ask: am I living a life mirroring societal, cultural, national and religious programming? Alternatively, am I consciously, every day, trying to jail break my divine spark from the prison of my lower self? The Freemason, engaged in the activity of mind science, constantly seeks to bring light to the dark aspects of his life and symbolically build his Temple — himself — into as perfect a being as can be.

The skull protects the most precious aspect of your self while in physical form: your brain. As such, it is the most valuable part of the human body, your own sanctum sanctorum.

No skull, no brain.

No brain, no life.

No life, no existence.

We need our skull while in physical form.

The representation of the skull, therefore, tells us that in our mortal human state the head is the seat of everything that keeps us alive, as it holds the brain. You can live with an artificial heart but there is no such thing as an artificial brain.

The brain is also the seat of consciousness, as consciousness emanates from the brain. As the seat of consciousness, it is believed the brain is the seat of the natural soul. According to French philosopher, mathematician and scientist, Rene Descartes, the pineal gland, located in the epithalamus, near the centre of the brain, is the seat of the natural soul, though this is debatable and a worthy topic for your further investigation.

The question we must ask now is: if the brain is the seat of consciousness, and it is through consciousness that we are physically alive, why not use an actual fleshy head instead of the skeleton of a skull in the symbol of the skull and crossbones?

The skull in the skull and crossbones teaches us that this group of bones, which housed the brain while alive, becomes an empty shell at death. It served its purpose to protect the brain during physical life but is no longer needed after physical death. If the soul is seated in the brain, and the brain is contained within the skull, then the left over shell tells us that in death the soul is set free from physical confinement.

In many ways, the lesson is similar to that of the cable tow detailed in an earlier chapter. The removal of the cable tow symbolically frees us from our attachment to material fears and thoughts of inadequacies. The death of the body, similarly, frees our soul from attachment to a material state. Remember, the soul is energy and energy never dies, it just relocates. As Albert Einstein said, 'Energy cannot be created or destroyed, it can only be changed from one form to another.' The skull teaches us that the energy of our soul no longer inhabits the physical self after death. The skull, once the house of the brain, the seat of the soul, is now an empty shell.

Okay, that's pretty morbid, you may be thinking.

In actuality, the skull teaches us to embrace life while we have it. It shouts to us, 'Hey! This is the place from which every thought emanates. This is where your brain sits. Your brain absorbs knowledge. The more positive knowledge you feed your brain, the more you feed your soul. The more you feed your soul, the healthier it becomes. Don't waste your life and leave behind an empty shell. Rather, leave behind a shell like the walls of a deserted classroom, where great lessons were absorbed. In death you graduate from the classroom to a higher life. Graduate with honours!'

The skull is a call to live life to the fullest. To enrich your soul with knowledge and amazing experiences. It is not a call to fear death.

Let's use the analogy of the classroom a little more. As a child, school is the totality of your life. Your friends are at school, your pastimes such as theatre, sports, the chess club, the year book, and the student newspaper all take place at school. Your first kiss occurs at school. You probably have a crush on one of your teachers. You fear detention. You hate Mr Greenburg's maths class. You thrive in Mr Kearney's literature class. You're the big shot on campus; the class clown, the jock, the nerd, or the quiet achiever. School is your world. The classroom is the centrality of your life.

When you leave school, you feel a little sad and a little scared. You leave behind the classroom and the campus grounds you know so well. The dozens of other kids you grew up with are suddenly scattered to the workforce or further education. The comforts of school, which you clung to for so long, are taken away. A part of your life is over, but life does not cease to exist – it simply changes from one form to another. From puberty to adulthood. From high school to university or the workforce. You are making an unavoidable yet necessary progression to the next phase of your personal evolution. What was once the very core of your being, the high school classroom, is now an empty shell in which you'd once sat. Likewise, at death, the skull – in which your brain, and thus your consciousness, once sat – becomes an empty shell. It served its purpose and served it well. This is the symbolism of the skull.

What then of the crossbones, of which there are two forming an X?

The two bones that form the crossbones are the femur bones.

Why is this? Why not two radial bones, two ribs, two humerus bones or two malleus bones?

The femur bones are located in the legs, specifically in the thighs. They are the bones closest to the centre of the body and are also the longest and strongest bones we have. The femur has long symbolised strength and power in that it can support 30 times the weight of a human adult and can resist forces of 1,800 to 2,500 pounds[103]. A human being cannot relocate his body without a femur bone.

At the top of the femur bone is a sphere known as the head. A sphere is a three-dimensional representation of a circle, which is the symbol of our spiritual nature, as the square is a symbol of our material nature. That the longest and strongest bone in the body is surmounted by a shape representing spirituality offers an indication as to the symbolic significance of the femur. That this bone also produces red blood cells through the cores of bone marrow in its head (in a process known as hematopoiesis), makes the femur an apt symbol of regeneration. Here then, in the spherical head of the femur we have the symbology of the intersection of the spiritual and the physical.

As the strongest bones in the body, located in the thighs, the femurs allow us to walk upright, thus separating humans from the animal kingdom. According to science, what makes us truly unique as humans and separates us from all other creatures is our capacity for rational thought (the brain, as mentioned above) and the ability to walk upright, represented by the femur.

The symbolism of the skull and crossbones tells us that as a physical being – and there are millions of non-human physical beings on the planet, from nanobes to blue whales – the human is the highest form of physical incarnation consciousness can inhabit. On Earth, in human form, there is no place higher a soul could aspire to inhabit. For our soul to grow to its greatest potential while inhabiting human form, it is necessary to garner knowledge (the brain in the skull) and to live a virtuous life walking justly and uprightly (the crossed femurs).

The femur bone is also synonymous with carnal desire, which is the lowest form of desire. What happens during sexual intercourse? You wrap your thighs around your partner, right? Hence, the femur is a symbol of lust and an apt symbol for man. After all, man is one of the few creatures that has sex for pleasure.

There are several references to thigh bones throughout the Bible. One of the more famous references occurs in the story of Jacob, who wrestled 'a man' (it was God) through the night until sunrise. What the story is really about is Jacob wrestling himself or, more specifically, wrestling his carnal desires, his animal nature. Jacob's problem had always been dependence on his own material and carnal desires instead of trusting in his higher self; his spiritual nature. Jacob wrestles with God all night until finally his thigh (femur) is put out. God asks Jacob to let him go and Jacob refuses to do so unless He blesses him. God blesses Jacob and Jacob names the place where he was blessed, Peniel, which translates as Face of God.

Does the word Peniel look familiar? Similar to 'pineal' as in pineal gland, right? And what is the pineal gland said to be? The seat of the soul and the means by which we connect to our spiritual self – the means by which we can see the face of God.

The story of Jacob, therefore, tells us that the thigh bone represents our base/animal/carnal self. When this base self is detached and we transcend our animal desires, we are be able to see the face of God, which is the divine spark at the centre of our soul. Through death, the femur (animal self) is detached from our existence.

The next question we must ask is: Why are the femurs crossed? Why is the symbol not of a skull upon two perpendicular femurs?

The symbol 'X' is a letter representing a changing quantity called a variable. X can be anything depending on the problem you are attempting to solve. For example: if one banana costs 10 pounds, then 10 bananas = X. What is X? In this case, X = 100 pounds — or some very expensive bananas!

To understand the variable, which is X, you must first understand the question. In the symbolism of the crossbones in the form of an X, to understand the equation of death you must first understand the question of life.

In numerology, X has a value of 24 and is the equivalent of the number 6 (24 = 2 + 4 = 6). Esoterically, the number 6 (hexad) is considered a 'number of Creation' because, as the Book of Genesis tells us, God created the world in six days.[104] In the aspect of human nature, 6 symbolises the principle of free will, spiritual harmony and the recognition of good and evil – all of which makes us human.

Six is represented by a hexagram or a six-pointed star, which consists of two interpenetrating triangles, one pointed up, the other pointed down. The hexagram represents the harmony of a union of opposites, such as male and female. It also represents the union of spiritual and physical, one triangle pointing to the material earth, the other to the spiritual heavens. Through spiritual knowledge, we ascend; through material-centric knowledge, we descend. The key to transcending our base self is to find unity, or harmony, in our physical and spiritual natures. It is little wonder the Pythagoreans considered 6 the perfection of all parts. As Manly P. Hall said, the number 6 is 'the form of forms, articulation of the universe and a doer of the soul.'

In the Hebrew alphabet, VAV is equal to the number six and denotes physical completion.[105] The word VAV means 'hook', which is not surprising in the current context as a femur bone with its spherical head looks a lot like a hook! VAV also means a nail or a tent peg, which along with a hook, connects one object to another. In grammar the VAV serves the same purpose as the word 'and', which connects one set of words in a sentence to another set of words in the same sentence. The VAV teaches us about connection to our inner self[106], and the connection we have to one another. Through life, we are also connected to death. Death is a different existence for the soul, which is energy and can never be destroyed.

In Roman numerals X is the number 10. Pythagoreans considered 10 a sacred number and a universal number signifying the full course of life. Francis Brett writes in *The Magus* (1801):

> 'For beyond that (10) we cannot number but by replication; and it either implies all numbers within itself, or explains them by itself, and its own, by multiplying them… As the number ten flows back into a unity, from whence it proceeded, so every thing that is flowing is returned back to that from which it had the beginning of its flux: so water returns to the sea, from whence it had its beginning; the body returns to the earth, from whence it was taken; time returns to eternity, from whence it flowed; the spirit shall return to God, who gave it.'[107]

Aetius, an Eclectic philosopher from Ancient Greece, wrote: 'Ten is the very nature of number. All Greeks and all barbarians alike count up to ten, and having reached ten revert again to the unity.'

The X of the crossbones also alludes to one final piece of symbolism – that of a perfect man. Where have you heard the term 'perfect man' or 'universal man'? In Leonardo Da Vinci's *Vitruvian Man*.

Da Vinci's *Vitruvian Man* is a drawing of a man with outstretched limbs touching the circumference of a circle and the edges of a square, with his navel falling in the exact centre of the circle.

The Vitruvian Man is based on the teachings of Marcus Vitruvius, the Roman architect, who was born about 80 BCE. Vitruvius authored a treatise on architecture entitled *De Architectura,* in which he discussed, among other things, the building of temples. Vitruvius detailed the proper symmetry and proportion required to build a temple, but not any old temple. The temple of Vitruvius' writing is a perfect temple, based on what he considers the perfect proportions of the human body, which are symmetrically drawn within both a circle and a square.

What other 'temple' can you think of that uses squares and circles and is a representation of the perfect man? A Masonic temple, otherwise known as the Masonic lodge room.

Da Vinci's *Vitruvian Man* is two superimposed images. In one image, the Vitruvian man stands with his arms and legs outstretched as a symbol of perfection and thus forms a letter X with his limbs – another representation of the crossbones and their symbolism of the aspiration we must have to perfect our human self, housing our soul, before death.

The other image of the Vitruvian Man is drawn standing upright, legs parallel to one another, but with an interesting positioning of the feet. The heel of the right foot forms a right angle with the inside of the left foot, thus creating a square. Now combine this square foot position with the position of the second superimposed man, whose legs are stretched out on a sixty-degree angle, and you effectively have a square superimposed on a compasses – the Masonic square and compasses logo.

Thus, the X of Da Vinci's *Vitruvian Man* tells us, as does the X of the crossbones, that a perfect man is achieved by a unity of the material (the square) and the spiritual (the compasses).

Next time you see a skull and crossbones, do not consider it a morbid emblem of mortality. It is not solely a 'Memento Mori'; a remembrance of death. You don't need to be reminded that you're going to die one day. You must be reminded to live.

Life is the symbolism of the skull and crossbones, not death. That bones stay in the Earth long after we die – the world's oldest fossilised human bones are more than 3.2 million years old! – is symbolic of living an earthly life that leaves an imprint on the world long after we're physically gone. Make your life count.

Life Application
Often misinterpreted as a grim symbol of death, the skull and crossbones is, in fact, a symbol of life, or more accurately, a call to live life justly, uprightly and to its fullest.

The skull is the place that once housed the brain, which is the most important organ in the human body. A person can stay alive with the replacement or removal of other organs – an artificial heart, a kidney transplant, a lung or liver removed – but one cannot live without a brain nor can the brain of one person be replaced with the brain of another.

The brain is also considered by some to be the seat of the soul. It is the house of the pineal gland, said to be a person's third eye by which one connects to their spiritual self, outside of their physical self.

The symbol here is of the skull and not the brain. This is to teach that although the brain is the centrality of your physical existence, it is not the completion of your existence. When the physical state dies, you are left with an empty shell of a skull in which the magnificent brain once operated. Sitting within this solid shell, the brain had limitations and, therefore, so too did the soul. The soul liberated from the physical body through death has no limitations. Your divine spark, that god-like essence of your self, has no limit.

The skull and crossbones is a call to live a life worth living. Make as much as you can of your life so as to leave your imprint on the earthly world when it is time for your soul to relocate to an existence without physical confinement.

ASK YOURSELF
- If I knew I was going to die tomorrow, how might I treat someone differently today?
- Am I afraid of death or do I embrace it?
- Am I living my life to the fullest?
- What can I do with my life today instead of waiting for tomorrow?
- Am I walking justly and uprightly in my dealings with people?
- Did I learn something new today?
- What imprint will I leave on the world when I'm gone?
- How will I be remembered? What will be written on my headstone?
- Is my fear of death affecting my ability to live life to its fullest?

Love rocks
The ashlars

Keep love in your heart. A life without it is like a sunless garden when the flowers are dead.

— Oscar Wilde

Every Masonic lodge room features a representation of two blocks of stone. One is a hunk of rough stone, unshaped and jagged edged, as if taken straight from a quarry or broken off the side of a mountain. The other is a refined stone, shaped into a perfect cube. These two stones are known as the rough ashlar and the perfect ashlar, and are two representations of the same stone.

The perfect ashlar is the rough ashlar transformed into a perfect geometrical shape by the use of various tools. The tools used to shape the stone are the same working tools presented to a Mason in the Entered Apprentice and Fellowcraft Degrees. They are the chisel, common gavel, 24-inch gauge, square, level and plumb.

Let's get a little lesson on stone shaping.

A stone is cut from the ground with a chisel, the rough edges chipped off with a gavel and the stone measured with a 24-inch gauge – the three tools of an Entered Apprentice. The stone is then crafted into a perfect cube by way of testing its perpendiculars with a plumb, its horizontals with a level and its corners exacted into right angles by use of a square – the three working tools of a Fellowcraft. Later in the building process, the cubed stone is placed perfectly within the final structure by means of a pencil with which the plans for the structure are drawn; a skirrett, which delineates the foundation; and compasses, which determines the structure's boundaries and circular aspects – the working tools of a Master Mason. The trowel, which is also a tool of the Master Mason, is used to spread the cement that holds each block firmly in place and binds one block to another.

Here then, in the complete working tools of Freemasonry, we have the operative tools with which to build any structure. The tools are used progressively from those that extract and shape the stone (the chisel and gavel) to those that measure the stone (the square, the level and the plumb), to those that at last fit the stone into the structure (the skirrett, the compasses, the pencil and the trowel).

Through progressive operative use of these tools, the stone is thus transformed from its crudest state as a rock extracted from the quarry into its perfect state as a cube – or from a rough ashlar to a perfect ashlar. Symbolically, the Mason uses his personal working tools progressively to shape himself from a crude state of existence into a perfect being, equal in all his sides – body, mind and soul; material, mental and spiritual – of which the six-faced cube is a representation.

What do I mean by a 'crude state of existence'?

The definition of 'crude' is: *in a raw or unprepared state; unrefined or natural.* We are all products of our environment born into a society that places the greatest importance on physicality, possessions and wealth. As such, we are naturally unrefined in the part of us we can't see or touch – our spiritual, higher self.

So I'm supposed to transform myself into some sort of all-knowing, dressed-in-white, happy and joyful spirit? Is that the point of all this?

For many, the thought of transcending their crude nature by working toward the illumination of their spiritual nature, or higher self, is a long process with no tangible result. As such, it's easy to sit back, rest on one's laurels and say, 'to hell with it!' A commitment to elevate yourself above your natural, crude nature, however, does not mean that you're going to transform yourself into the next Mother Teresa or Gandhi. The end of this journey does not result in canonisation. The process of life is about taking baby steps up a winding stairway. Improving yourself one step at a time is a method of ascending beyond your crude nature. How?

- Be nicer to a neighbour today than you were to that neighbour yesterday

- Spend thirty minutes more on education this week than you did the last
- Reduce your spending on possessions you don't really need
- Smile more than you did yesterday
- Change a negative thought into a positive thought
- Help someone today without expecting anything in return
- Block negativity from entering into your thoughts
- Identify how much time you waste in a day and eliminate the waste
- Genuinely listen to someone during a conversation. Don't simply concentrate on figuring out what you're going to say next. Listen to absorb, don't listen to reply
- Show empathy toward someone in a worse position than you
- Exercise
- Set aside time for meditation. This doesn't mean sitting cross-legged on the floor chanting 'AUM'. Rather make quiet time for yourself while taking a hot shower or enjoying a solitary walk and go inside yourself, into your thoughts. Channel positivity about your life and the lives of those around you.
- Think of a negative aspect of your life and cast a mental white light over it.
- Enjoy the moment, right now. Don't focus on the past – you can never re-live it
- Don't get caught up in the future – it never comes. Whatever you are doing now, do it to your best ability and with your greatest attention
- Don't expend energy trying to control others. Control yourself, curb your own passions and lusts.
- Make a daily list of everything you're grateful for.
- Keep a log of your mental chatter and figure out the positive and negative direction of your thoughts and how you can steer towards greater positivity.
- Try to feel a connection of love with a complete stranger.
- Sharpen your brain today. Read a challenging book; construct a puzzle; commit passages of text, song lyrics or a poem to memory (you will be amazed at how memory work sharpens your mind – another 'secret' of Freemasonry)

The word 'crude' is further defined as: *lacking finish, polish or completeness.* Lacking polish translates well into the lesson of the ashlars. The rough ashlar, hewn from the quarry, lacks polish. Only through a time-consuming process does the unpolished rough ashlar transform into a finished and polished perfect ashlar. Only a finished stone is fit for placement in a structure. Any building made of unfinished stones, that is, stones with rough corners or poor shaping, will not stand the test of time, and is destined to fall apart.

If we are each made in the image of God – a higher intelligence, a divine source

– then it serves to reason that there is a part of us that is perfection. We are all created from the same source energy. Beneath the pain, limitations, sadness, anger, protective shields and misconceptions of our physicality, is our divine spark. This divine spark is eternal and is our direct connection to a higher power.

Being born into a human state, we are flawed creatures from the outset. Only when those flaws are chipped away and removed by use of our symbolic working tools do we transform our flawed self (rough ashlar) into a perfect self (perfect ashlar). We are not looking to build something new from scratch but rather to remove the superficial exterior – those rough edges – and reveal the perfection hidden somewhere deep inside of us. As Michelangelo said, 'Every block of stone has a statue inside it and it is the task of the sculptor to discover it.

Inside each of us is a divine spark, our connection to the source, the location of which is our task to discover.

The cube (perfect ashlar) represents our perfect state. Why is this? Why not a rectangle or an orb? To understand the symbolism of the perfect ashlar we must first understand the properties of a cube.

A cube is a solid bounded by six equal squares, the angle between any two adjacent faces being a right angle. In a cube, three of the faces (or sides) meet at each vertex. In elementary geometry, a cube is known as a type of polyhedron, which is a solid in three dimensions with flat faces, straight edges and sharp vertices or corners. The technical name for a cube is a hexahedron, as it is composed of six faces. The various polyhedrons include the tetrahedron, composed of four triangular faces, three of which meet at a vertex; an octahedron, composed of eight triangular faces; and a dodecahedron, composed of twelve pentagonal faces.

The cube is one of the five perfect solids of Euclidean geometry – also known as Platonic solids – and has for centuries been used as a religious symbol. In the Book of Revelation, the New Jerusalem that allegorically descends from heaven is in the shape of a cube. The holiest site in Islam, the Kaaba at Mecca,which Muslims face during prayer, is a cuboid structure. According to tradition, the Kaaba was built by Abraham and was the first house built by man to worship God, making it the first and oldest mosque in history.[108]

Esoterically, the cube is a symbol of the regenerated and perfected soul, living in a state of permanence.[109] The three dimensional cube emanates from the two dimensional square. As the square is not a shape found in nature, it represents the material. A square has four sides, symbolic of the four states of matter – earth (solid), water (liquid), air (gas), fire (plasma) – and of the four stages of human development – childhood, youth, manhood and old age.

Okay, so that's the basics of the cube, but here's the kicker. If you unfold a cube-shaped box and flatten it out, a Latin cross is formed. To the ancients, the four arms of the cross represented the four elements. The cross was venerated as a symbol long before its popularisation by the Christian Church; however it is through the Christian Church that the symbolic cross is most well-known.

You know the story of Jesus Christ and his crucifixion upon the cross. Do you remember how Pontius Pilate placed the letters INRI at the top of Jesus' cross? Common Christian teaching tells us that the letters stand for *Iesvs Nazarenvs Rex Iudaeorvm*, which is Latin for *Jesus of Nazareth, King of the Jews*. Scottish Rite Masonry, which uses the cube-to-cross unfolding as a key part of its symbolism, teaches that the letters INRI actually stand for *Igne Natura Renovatur Integra – All Nature is Renewed by Fire*.

Pure matter is restored by spirit.

When we free ourselves of the chains of the material world (our crude nature) and find the divine spark within us, our connection to the centre is restored. You become what you were intended to be – god-like. You don't become God, but god-like. After all, the Bible tells us that God made man in his own image. Find the fire that burns in your belly, through the pursuit of truth and love, and you will be spiritually regenerated. This is the symbolism of the cross and thus of the cube, or perfect ashlar.

Here then we have the deep symbolic meaning of the rough and perfect ashlars, remembering that these two blocks of stone are the same stone in two different forms, just as you are a soul within a human body. Do you see the correspondence? Your physical and spiritual are two states connected and operating as one.

Through a well-governed life in pursuit of continual betterment, you can overcome your material/animal/crude nature. You can chip away at the rough edges and shape your rough ashlar into a perfect cube. This is the aim of Freemasonry, and the purpose of the Masonic working tools and other symbols. Let me break it down for you even further:

By curbing the ego and bridling your base passions (the compasses) you chip away at the roughness of your character (common gavel). This is done through an educational process (chisel) and takes time to achieve (24-inch gauge). At the beginning, you will not be able to see the end result or destination, but you must have faith that you will get there (the winding stairs).

By walking uprightly (plumb), living in harmony with others (the beehive), treating others with equality (level), adhering to the Universal Law (the mosaic pavement), and understanding that your every thought and action is recorded (pencil) on a higher plane, you will achieve a union of your material and spiritual natures (square / square and compasses) that will provide illumination (the apron) and lead you to the divine spark at your centre (point within a circle).

The cube unfolds into a cross, which is constructed by two intersecting planes. This is the intersection of your physical and spiritual selves, just as the vertex of the square – the meeting point of the horizontal and the perpendicular – represents a fusion of the body and soul, the human state and the higher self. Your aim should be to link your human self with your spiritual self, which you have forgotten or neglected. This is the supreme knowledge, attainment of which is the right of every person. It is the point within the circle of Freemasonry; the Buddha-nature of Buddhism; the inner spark taught by the Jewish mystics; the candle flame burning in a niche in the wall of God's temple in the Koran; the Kingdom of God within you, as preached by Jesus; the inner light of Quaker belief; the Hindi Brahm Gyan (Divine Knowledge); and the Akhu of the Ancient Egyptians.

The cross takes the shape of a man with outstretched arms, and the intersection of these two planes takes place at the section of the cross that corresponds to the chest.

What is located in your chest? Your heart.

What does your heart symbolically represent? Love.

What is the key to finding your divine spark? Love.

In 2013, *The Guardian* website published an article entitled 'What is Love? Five theories on the greatest emotion of all'.[110] According to the article, 'What is love?' was the most searched phrase on Google in 2012. The article asked writers from the fields of science, psychotherapy, literature, religion and philosophy to give their definition of love.

> The theoretical physicist said love is a powerful neurological condition.
> The psychotherapist said there are six kinds of love.
> The philosopher said love is commitment, passion and nurturing.
> The romantic novelist said love is the driver for all great stories.
> The nun said love is life's greatest blessing.
> They are all correct.

Life Application

We are souls inhabiting human form, and as such are subject to the flaws of being human. Inside each of us is a divine spark, which is a perfect part of ourselves. It is unblemished, eternal, pure love. The divine spark is the god-like part of us. To connect with your divine spark is to connect to the source, the Universe, the centre; to God, the Holy Spirit, the life force.

The divine spark is your perfect ashlar, your most beautiful self, your ultimate you. However, this perfect ashlar is hidden inside our flesh and bone, symbolically inside of our material nature, our crudest self. Use your symbolic working tools to smooth out the rough edges of your animal nature and reveal the perfect ashlar deep inside of you.

Your perfect ashlar is deemed a perfect cube through measurement performed by a square, that is, a perfect right angle, the joining of a horizontal and a vertical. We are born on the horizontal, which is our material make up. We must attain the vertical, that is, we must become upright of our own doing. Only when we raise our vertical can it join with our horizontal and form a right angle. The symbolic idea here is that the vertical side represents one aspect, the horizontal side another aspect, and the hypotenuse is offspring of the combined sides. The combination of one and the other produces a new form of being altogether. When we combine our body with our mind, we enrich our soul and become more enlightened beings as a result of living an upright life.

How can you live an upright life? Here are a few tips to get you started:

1. Acknowledge your faults and change your attitude to adjust them.
You can only change your life when you know which parts of your life need changing. Awareness is the beginning of change. Be aware of yourself and your actions. As Lao Tzu said, 'He who knows others is wise. He who knows himself is enlightened.'

A good definition of self-awareness is our capacity to be aware of our traits and behaviours, and to have conscious knowledge of our own character, feelings, motives, and desires.

Until you are aware in the moment of the controls to your thoughts, emotions, words, and behaviour, you will have difficulty making changes in your life and its direction.

2. Try to transcend your material nature.
This is a difficult but achievable goal. To begin your pursuit of transcendence, try to put people ahead of material objects. Next time you spend money on something, ask yourself if you really need it in your life or if that money is better spent on developing a relationship with another person. Buying a cup of coffee for a friend, especially a friend in need, is money well spent.

Don't think for a moment that I'm telling you to get rid of all your money and worldly possessions. One can have a large bank account and still pursue transcendence above their material nature. Take the Biblical example of Job.

Job was one of the most upright and honest men you'll find in the Bible. He made good choices, he served God (that is, he served his higher nature) and he tried his best to resist temptation. He had strong moral fibre. He wasn't a poor monk who spent time meditating in caves. In fact, Job was rich; really rich! The Bible tells us he 'owned seven thousand sheep, three thousand camels, five hundred yoke of oxen and five hundred donkeys, and had a large number of servants.' He was the equivalent to a modern-day billionaire! He did not let his wealth corrupt him, however. He chose to better himself above material possessions.

Remember, it is not money or power that corrupts. It is the love of either above a love of our inner self that makes the drink poison.

3. Read, read and read some more - keep feeding your mind.
English writer Joseph Addison (1672-1719) wrote that, 'Reading is to the mind what exercise is to the body.'

Rene Descartes said, 'The reading of all good books is like a conversation with the finest minds of past centuries.'

Reading is learning. Someone once told me that libraries exist to make us all feel incredibly stupid. All the knowledge of all the ages is at our fingertips, contained in books.

Hundreds of books are available that offer instructions on how to smooth out your rough ashlar. The books of almost any religion or belief system offer lessons on how to live a good life. They include, the Bible, the Torah, the Koran, The Book of Mormon, The Golden Verses of Pythagoras, the Vedas, the Jain Agamas, *A Course in Miracles*, the *Tao Te Ching*, *The Art of Happiness*, and *The Essential Gandhi*.

There are great novels, too, that deliver moral messages, such as: *Watership Down*, *To Kill a Mockingbird*, *Dune*, and even the *Harry Potter* series.

4. Change yourself a little at a time.
Change does not occur overnight. Knock at the door of change and greater knowledge. Allow the door to be opened to you. Don't shut out change, embrace it.

Take an honest look at what's going on in your personal, professional and spiritual life, and make changes.

5. Understand the Universal Law, the Golden Rule, and enact it in all you do.
The heart of the Universal Law, known more commonly as The Golden Rule, exists in every great teaching system. Confucius phrased it perfectly 500 years before Jesus when he said: 'Never impose on others what you would not choose for yourself.'

The Hindu rule of Dharma states: 'One should never do that to another which one regards as injurious to one's own self'

In the Baha'i Faith it is written: 'Ascribe not to any soul that which thou wouldst not have ascribed to thee, and say not that which thou doest not.'

6. Strive to live a quiet life.
A quiet life doesn't mean becoming a recluse and living under a waterfall in a state of permanent meditation. Rather you should learn to quiet your mind to greed, lust, selfishness, hatred, theft, murder, cheating and lying – the rough edges of your ashlar. Also keep a tongue of good report.

7. Practice what you preach.
Don't tell others to do something you are not willing to do yourself.

Jesus gives a good example in Matthew 7: 3-5 when he says: 'Why do you look at the speck of sawdust in your brother's eye and pay no attention to the plank in your own eye? How can you say to your brother, 'Let me take the speck out of your eye,' when all the time there is a plank in your own eye? You hypocrite, first take the plank out of your own eye, and then you will see clearly to remove the speck from your brother's eye.'

Ask Yourself
- If love became the national currency, how wealthy would I be?
- When was the last time I said 'I love you' to myself?
- What is worth smiling about right now?
- Am I committed to pleasing others at the sacrifice of myself?
- Did my actions today adhere to the Golden Rule?
- What do I like in life and what do I love in life? How can I turn my likes into my loves?
- What makes me come alive? What sets me on fire?
- Do I practice what I preach?

Putting it all into practice
Internalising the external

Having knowledge but lacking the power to express it clearly is no better than never having any ideas at all.

— Pericles

Here you are, in the final pages. You've read every chapter and studied the life application of each symbol. If you truthfully answered the questions asked, you've already developed a better knowledge of yourself than you had before reading this book. Now there is just one question left: how do you put all you have learned into practice?

Freemasonry is an external method of improving the internal part of yourself. Freemasonry is a method of unlocking the doorways in your consciousness that allow you to discover your enormous potential. If you're seeking bigger muscles, increased flexibility, greater core strength, better hair, a cleaner colon or the accumulation of material wealth, Freemasonry has no answers. If you want to become a better person through the development of good morals and virtues, the teachings of Freemasonry offer a winding staircase. To climb this winding staircase is a choice only you can make.

There's an old saying that when you throw your heart over the wall, the mind and body follow. This is certainly the case in Masonic instruction. If your heart possesses a desire, a want, a need to become a better person, the rest of you will follow. When you walk a path to becoming a better person today than you were yesterday, you cannot possibly end up on the wrong side of the tracks. If you follow the lessons of the external symbols of Freemasonry, and learn to internalise these lessons, your spiritual evolution is inevitable. This spiritual evolution will enable you to know yourself better. Absorption of knowledge is beneficial, but true higher intelligence is reached through the internalisation of knowledge and practical use.

Internalisation takes place when something you know becomes something you believe in and live by. You can read the words and attain the knowledge, but it is only when the knowledge is applied that wisdom is attained.

It is better to be the wisest person in the room than the smartest. The smart man lists every Masonic symbol and how they could improve himself; the wise man *uses* every Masonic symbol to improve himself. Once you apply new knowledge as an undeniable truth that must be acted upon, you achieve wisdom.

The knowledge you have attained through reading this book may be difficult to comprehend at first. In fact, your mind may initially protest much of what you have read here. Such a reaction is to be expected. Human nature rejects change and protests internalisation of new knowledge because we have been programmed our entire lives to think and act differently. You once thought within the limitations of material/physical experiences but as you have seen through the lessons presented in this book, there is a whole other reality in which you exist – the spiritual reality.

To study Masonic symbolism solely as an intellectual pursuit places restrictions on the extent of your education. You are encouraged to study how Masonic symbols can empower your life as an intellectual pursuit, but also to go further and meditate on the symbols in order to understand them through direct experience. Intellectual knowledge is healthy, but personal growth is attained through experiential knowledge. As you study these symbols, ingest them and apply them to your daily living, remember that Freemasonry is a science of awakening consciousness and a process of improvement. That which we experience with our consciousness, we never forget. There is only so much that can be learned by reading a book. True knowledge, which results in personal growth, comes from experience. This experience is wholly personal. Freemasonry is an experience of the heart, mind and soul, and no man can make claim to know the heart, mind and soul of another.

Accept the idea that you are not limited to your material, physical experiences but also exist in the spiritual reality. The symbols of Freemasonry are the embodiment of ideas emanating from a higher plane. When applied to internal use, they serve to smooth your rough ashlar, empower your soul and reveal the divine spark at your centre, thus purging your lower nature so that you can manifest your higher, true self. In this way, you truly get to know yourself.

APPENDIX A

FAMOUS FREEMASONS

From presidents to pop stars, actors, astronauts, entrepreneurs, authors and athletes, Freemasonry attracts members from all professions. The history of Freemasonry contains a plethora of famous names. Here are a few of them.

Bud Abbot, of Abbot and Costello fame, was an active Freemason and Shriner, and a member of Daylite Lodge No. 525 in Michigan.

At the time of the lunar landing, **Buzz Aldrin** was a member of Clear Lake Lodge No. 1417, Seagate, Texas. In the wake of Aldrin's space mission, the Grand Lodge of Texas formed Tranquillity Lodge No. 2000, named after Tranquillity Base, the location of Apollo 11's landing site.

American Revolutionary War General, **Benedict Arnold** was a member of Hiram Lodge No. 1, New Haven, Connecticut.

Mel Blanc, the voice of Bugs Bunny, Daffy Duck and other Looney Tunes characters, joined the Order of DeMolay as a boy, and was a Freemason for 50 years.

The late Oscar winner, **Ernest Borgnine**, was initiated into Abingdon Lodge No.48, California, and there is evidence that he was also a member of Melrose Lodge No.63 in California.

Sir Winston Churchill, one of the greatest leaders of the 20th century, was a member of Studholme Alliance No.1591 and Rosemary Lodge No.285, where he was made a Master Mason in 1902.

Legendary Hollywood film director, **Cecille B. DeMille,** was a member of Prince of Orange Lodge No.16, New York City.

President Gerald Ford was initiated into Freemasonry on 30 September 1949 within the Temple of Malta Lodge No.465, Grand Rapids, Michigan. He was made a courtesy Master Mason of Columbia Lodge No.3, Washington, D.C. on 18 May 1951. He later said in 1975, "When I took my obligation as a Master Mason (incidentally, with my three younger brothers), I recalled the value my own father attached to that Order. But I had no idea that I would ever be added to the company of the Father of our Country [George Washington] and 12 other members of the Order who also served as Presidents of the United States."

Benjamin Franklin held the Masonic title of Grand Master of Pennsylvania, and was one of the 13 Freemasons who signed the American Constitution. In February

1731, Benjamin Franklin was recorded as a member of St. John's Lodge, Philadelphia.

President Theodore Roosevelt was a member of Matinecock Lodge No. 806 of Oyster Bay, NY.

Oscar winning actor **Clark Gable** was raised to the Sublime Degree of Master Mason in Beverly Hills Lodge No.528, California.

Oliver Hardy of Laurel and Hardy fame was a Freemason in Solomon Lodge No. 20, Florida

Authors **Sir Arthur Conan Doyle**, **Mark Twain** and **Oscar Wilde** were all Freemasons.

Harry Houdini was immensely proud of his Masonic affiliations. The magician was a member of the York Rite and became a Shriner just before his untimely death at the age of 52 from peritonitis. Harry Houdini was initiated into Freemasonry on 21st August 1923 in St. Cecile Lodge No. 568, New York.

Jungle Book author **Rudyard Kipling** was initiated into Hope and Perseverance Lodge No. 782 in Lahore, India. He later wrote to *The Times of London*, "I was Secretary for some years of the Lodge ... which included Brethren of at least four creeds. I was entered [as an Apprentice] by a member from Brahmo Somaj, a Hindu, passed [to the degree of Fellow Craft] by a Mohammedan, and raised [to the degree of Master Mason] by an Englishman. Our Tyler was an Indian Jew."

American pioneer aviator, **Charles Lindbergh**, received his Masonic degrees at Keystone Lodge No.243, in St. Louis, Missouri.

US Army General **Douglas McArthur** was a member of Manila Lodge No.1 in the Philippines.

Golf legend **Arnold Palmer** is a member of Loyalhanna Lodge No.275 in Latrobe, Pennsylvania.

King of the Cowboys **Roy Rogers** was a member of Hollywood Lodge No.355, California. The cross and his 33rd Degree Scottish Rite emblem is displayed on his gravestone.

Warner Brothers founder **Harry Warner** was a member of Mount Olive Lodge No. 506, California.

Legendary actor **John Wayne** was a member of Marion McDaniel Lodge No. 56, Tucson, Arizona and also a 33rd Degree Scottish Rite Mason.

Oscar Wilde attended Apollo University Lodge No. 357, Oxford (UGLE).

World boxing champion, **Sugar Ray Robinson**, was a member of Prince Hall affiliated lodge Joppa No. 55, New York City.

English cricketer **Herbert Sutcliffe** was a Freemason as is West Indies cricket legend**, Sir Clive Lloyd.**

Australian cricketing icon, **Sir Donald Bradman**, was initiated into Lodge Tarbolton No. 12 in 1929. Other cricketers including **Bill Lawry, Bill Ponsford** and **Bobby Simpson** were also Freemasons.

The inventor of Vegemite, **Fred Walker**, was a Freemason as was **Thomas Mayne**, the inventor of Milo.

Several British Monarchs were Freemasons, including: **King George IV** (1762 - 1830)**, King William IV** (1765 - 1837)**, King Edward VII** (1841 - 1910)**, King Edward VIII** (1894 - 1972) **and King George VI** (1895 - 1952).

Comedian **Richard Pryor** was made a Mason at Henry Brown Lodge No. 22 in Peoria, Illinois.

Actor **Peter Sellers** was raised to the Sublime Degree of Master Mason in 1951 in Chelsea Lodge No. 3098, the same lodge as his father.

Australia's 'King of Television', actor **Graham Kennedy**, was a member of Lodge of St. Kilda.

Country and Western star, **Brad Paisley**, is a member of Hiram Lodge No. 4 in Franklin, Tennessee and a 32nd Degree Scottish Rite Mason.

UFC fighters, **Guy Mezger, Ryan Jimmo** and **Pat Miletich** are all Freemasons.

Basketballers **Scottie Pippen** and **Shaquille O'Neal** are Freemasons, as is American footballer **John Elway**.

Michael Richards, who played 'Kramer' on Seinfeld, is a Freemason at Culver City-Foshay Lodge No. 467 in Culver City, California.

APPENDIX B

THE THREE MASONIC DEGREES

The three Masonic degrees are designed to represent the three stages of life: youth, adulthood and old age. Each degree teaches important moral and spiritual lessons.

Entered Apprentice
1st Degree
The Entered Apprentice degree represents youth. The three working tools of this degree are the twenty-four inch gauge, the common gavel and the chisel.

The Entered Apprentice degree teaches the importance of secrecy, keeping one's word, truth, charity to all mankind, and the attainment of knowledge.

Fellowcraft
2nd Degree
The Fellowcraft represents adulthood. The three working tools of this degree are the square, level and plumb.

The Fellowcraft degree teaches the importance of commitment, obeying rules and laws, helping others, advancing education to cover the Seven Liberal Arts and Sciences, and hard work.

Sublime Degree of Master Mason
3rd Degree
The Master Mason represents old age. The three working tools of this degree are the pencil, compasses and skirrett. In American Masonry, the trowel is the working tool of this degree.

The Master Mason degree teaches the importance of loyalty, dedication, living a life of virtue and morality, and commitment to the work. Master Masons are taught to embrace life and not fear death.

Footnotes

Introduction – *pages 9-14*

1. http://en.wikipedia.org/wiki/Seven_Sages_of_Greece#cite_note-2 date accessed 14/02/2015
2. Wilmshurst, W. L., *The Meaning of Masonry*, Lund, Humphries & Co., LTD, Bradford and London, 1922, p. 95

How symbolism works – *pages 23-26*

3. http://www.cracked.com/photoplasty_875_25-symbols-you-never-noticed-in-everyday-life/ accessed 30/08/2015
4. http://www.masonic-lodge-of-education.com/freemason-symbols.html accessed 18/07/2015
5. Jung, C. J., *Man and His Symbols*, Dell Publishing, USA, 1964, p. 20

The Divine spark – You're a Real G – *pages 27-32*

6. The letter 'G' is not placed in the Square and Compasses in all Masonic jurisdictions. It is most prevalent in American Freemasonry.
7. New Thought, or Higher Thought, promotes the ideas that God, or a Higher Intelligence, is everywhere and the true human self is divine
8. Seton, J. *The Psychology of the Solar Plexus and Subconscious Mind*, Edward. J. Clode, New York, 1914, p. 14
9. Dumont, T. Q., *The Solar Plexus Or Abdominal Brain*, Advanced Thought Publishing, Chicago, 1920, p. 10
10. Pike, A., *Morals & Dogma of the Ancient and Accepted Scottish Rite of Freemasonry,* Supreme Council of the 33rd Degree for the Southern Jurisdiction of the United States, Charleston, 1871, p 854
11. , *The Lost Keys of Freemasonry*, Dover Publications, New York, 1923, p 64

Real men wear aprons – *pages 40-48*

12. Haywood, H. L., *Symbolical Masonry*, George H. Doran Company, New York, 1923
13. http://physics.about.com/od/lightoptics/a/vislightspec.htm accessed 11/07/16
14. Judd, D. B., *Colour in Business Science and Industry (Wiley Series in Pure and Applied Optics)*, Wiley-Qnterscience; 3 edition, 1975
15. http://en.wikipedia.org/wiki/Theosophy accessed 08/04/2015
16. http://blavatskytheosophy.com/the-sevenfold-nature-of-man/ accessed 08/04/2015
17. http://blavatskytheosophy.com/the-sevenfold-nature-of-man/ accessed 08/04/2015
18. Hartmann, F., *The Life of Philippus Theophrastus Bombast of Hohenheim: Known by the Name of Paracelsus, and the Substance of His Teachings Concerning Cosmology, Anthropology, Pneumatology ... Extracted and Translated from His Rare and Extensive Works and from Some Unpublished Manuscripts*, London, 1896, p 129

19 Not every jurisdiction requires its members to wear their aprons as such. The positioning of the apron flap is most prominently taught in American Freemasonry. English and Australian Freemasonry does not reposition the apron flap, which is worn pointed down for all degrees.

It's your time – the 24in Gauge – *pages 59-56*

20 Craft Masonry, also known as Blue Lodge Masonry, consists of three degrees: Entered Apprentice (1st degree); Fellowcraft (2nd degree) and Master Mason (3rd degree). Appendage bodies such as the Scottish Rite and York Rite confer degrees of a higher numerical value, but not of a higher symbolic value. The highest degree any Mason can achieve is that of the third degree, the full name of which is The Sublime Degree of Master Mason.

21 The Seven Liberal Arts & Sciences: Grammar, Rhetoric, Logic, Arithmetic, Geometry, Music, and Astronomy

22 Pike, A., *Morals & Dogma of the Ancient and Accepted Scottish Rite of Freemasonry*, Supreme Council of the 33rd Degree for the Southern Jurisdiction of the United States, Charleston, 1871, p34

23 http://www.nigms.nih.gov/Education/Pages/Factsheet_CircadianRhythms.aspx accessed 25/04/2015

24 http://www.nigms.nih.gov/Education/Pages/Factsheet_CircadianRhythms.aspx accessed 25/04/2015

25 http://www.exactlywhatistime.com/biological-clock/ accessed 25/04/2015

26 http://en.wikipedia.org/wiki/Suprachiasmatic_nucleus accessed 25/04/2015

27 http://en.wikipedia.org/wiki/Zeitgeber accessed 25/04/2015

28 http://www.exactlywhatistime.com/biological-clock/ accessed 25/04/2015

Keep chipping away – the Common Gavel – *pages 57-63*

29 http://www.gizapyramid.com/measurements.htm accessed 20/03/2016

30 Hancock, G., *Fingerprints of the Gods*, Three Rivers Press, New York, 1995

31 Hancock, G., *Fingerprints of the Gods*, Three Rivers Press, New York, 1995

32 Original name Xun Kuang. Xun Zi (also spelled Hsun-tze) was one of the three great Confucian philosophers of the classical period in China

What's the point? – the Point within a Circle – *pages 64-72*

33 Mackey, A. G., *The Symbolism of Freemasonry Illustrating and Explaining Its Science and Philosophy, its Legends, Myths and Symbols*, South Carolina, 1882, Chapter XV

34 Dermott, L., *Ahiman Rezon, or a help to all that are or would be Free and Accepted Masons Containing the Quintessence of all that has been Published on the subject of Freemasonry*, Leon Hyneman, Philadelphia, 1855

The bouncer at the door of your mind – the Tyler – *pages 73-81*

35 Robson, T., *An Introduction to Complementary Medicine*, Allen & Unwin, 2004, p 90

36 http://www.prevention.com/mind-body/emotional-health/stress-can-affect-heart-health accessed 22/03/2016

37 Tolkein, J. R. R., *The Lord of the Rings Part One the Fellowship of the Rings*,

Ballantine Books, New York, 1905

38 Tolle, E., *A New Earth Awakening Your Life's Purpose*, Penguin, North America, 2005

All a buzz – the Beehive – *pages 82-89*

39 http://www.funtrivia.com/en/subtopics/Stinging-Tales-From-Around-the-Globe-322070.html accessed 18/02/2015

40 http://en.wikipedia.org/wiki/Porphyry_(philosopher) accessed 18/02/2015

41 http://andrewgough.co.uk/articles_bee1/ accessed 18/02/2015

42 http://www.honey-health.com/honey-egypt/ accessed 18/02/2015

43 http://www.3838.co.jp/english/mitsubachi_park/frombeefarm/from05_rokkaku/index.html accessed 18/02/2015

44 http://earthsky.org/earth/why-do-bees-die-after-they-sting-you accessed 18/02/2015

45 Steinmatz, G.H., *Freemasonry: Its Hidden Meaning*, Macoy Publishing & Masonic Supply Co., Richmond, 1948, Chapter 12

46 Pike, A., *Morals & Dogma of the Ancient and Accepted Scottish Rite of Freemasonry,* Supreme Council of the 33rd Degree for the Southern Jurisdiction of the United States, Charleston, 1871, p 106

47 Ibid, p 108

48 Zain, C. C., *Ancient Masonry: The Spiritual Meaning of Masonic Degrees, Rituals and Symbols*, The Church of Light Rev. 2 ed, 1994 p 134

49 http://www.todayifoundout.com/index.php/2010/12/10-amazzzzing-bee-facts-infographic/ accessed 20/03/2015

50 http://www.buzzaboutbees.net/honey-bee-facts.html accessed 20/03/2015

51 http://insects.about.com/od/antsbees wasps/a/10-facts-honey-bees.htm accessed 04 / 03 / 2015

The only way is up – winding staircase – *pages 90-99*

52 Pike, A., *Morals & Dogma of the Ancient and Accepted Scottish Rite of Freemasonry,* Supreme Council of the 33rd Degree for the Southern Jurisdiction of the United States, Charleston, 1871, p 854

53 http://en.wikipedia.org/wiki/Jerome_Bruner date accessed 04 / 03 / 2015

54 Beck, M.; Geoghegan, R., *The Art of Proof: Basic Training for Deeper Mathematics,* Springer, New York: 2010

55 Sigler,S., *Fibonacci's Liber Abaci: A Translation into Modern English of Leonardo Pisano's Book of Calculation (Sources and Studies in the History of Mathematics and Physical Sciences),* Springer, New York, 2003

56 Goonatilake, S., *Toward a Global Science*, Indiana University Press, Indiana, 2008, p. 126

57 Mackey, A., *Encyclopaedia of Freemasonry and its Kindred Sciences,* Masonic History Company, USA, 1873

58 Kainz,H. P., *Natural Law: An Introduction and Re-examination*, Open Court Publishing, Chicago, 2004, p 6

59 Gensler, H. J., *Formal Ethics*. Routledge, New York, 1996

60 http://www.totalpresence.org/universal-laws.php date accessed 10/04/2015

61 http://www.brainyquote.com/quotes/quotes/w/winstonchu138235.html date accessed 10/04/ 2015

62 http://www.brainyquote.com/quotes/quotes/c/cslewis131286.html date accessed 10/04/2015

63 Mackey, A. G., *The Symbolism of Freemasonry Illustrating and Explaining Its Science and Philosophy, its Legends, Myths and Symbols,* South Carolina, 1882, Chapter XXVI

64 The Parable of the Talking Twins, also known as 'Do You Know Mother?' is accredited to Hungarian writer Útmutató a Léleknek

Black and white – the Mosaic Pavement – *pages 100-107*

65 http://jbq.jewishbible.org/assets/Uploads/362/362_duality.pdf date accessed 07/07/2015

66 https://en.wikipedia.org/wiki/Hermes_Trismegistus date accessed 22/03/2016

67 *The Kybalion, A Study of The Hermetic Philosophy of Ancient Egypt and Greece by Three Initiates* was first published in 1908 by a group of persons under the pseudonym of 'the Three Initiates' It claims to be the essence of the teachings of Hermes Trismegistus

68 http://altered-states.net/barry/newsletter420/ date accessed 22/03/2016

69 Bro. John K. Johnston, The Mosaic Pavement, http://www.hamiltondistrictcmasons.org/upload/lecture_file87.pdf date accessed 01/04/2015

70 Sickels, D., *The General Ahiman Rezon and Freemason's Guide,* Masonic Publishing and Manufacturing Co, New York, 1868, p 57

Ssssh – silence and secrecy – *pages 108-117*

71 http://www.masonicdictionary.com/bonebox.html date accessed 22/03/2016

72 Mackey, A. G., *An Encyclopedia of Freemasonry And Its Kindred Sciences,* Louis H Everts & Co, 1884 p 394

73 http://biblehub.com/isaiah/22-22.htm date accessed 22/03/2016

74 http://biblehub.com/isaiah/22-22.htm date accessed 22/03/2016

75 Watkins-Pitchford, Major R., *The Predominant Wish: A Masonic Study,* Lodge of Living Stones Library 2nd edition, 2011

76 Calcott, W., *A Candid Disquisition of the Principles and Practices of the Most Ancient and Honorable Society of Free and Accepted Masons,* Gale ECCO, 2007

77 Mackey, A. G., *An Encyclopedia of Freemasonry And Its Kindred Sciences,* Louis H Everts & Co, 1884 p 676

78 https://en.wikipedia.org/wiki/Symeon_the_New_Theologian, date accessed 04/04/2015

79 http://www.masonicdictionary.com/secrecy.html date accessed 31/10/2015

80 http://www.portsmouthaasr.com/sr4.htm date accessed 18/07/2015

81 http://phoenixmasonry.org/great_teachings_of_masonry.htm date accessed 22/03/2015

82 Freeman, L. OSB, *The Eucharist and Silence,* Lecture at the School of Prayer Archdiocese of Melbourne, 20th April 2005

83 Short Talk Bulletin - Jan. 1927, Masonic Service Association of North America

The Universe's Google – the pencil – *pages 118-125*

84 The pencil is one of the working tools of English Emulation Masonry and jurisdictions including Australia and Scotland. American Masonry does not use the pencil as a working tool in any degree.

85 http://searchengineland.com/by-the-numbers-twitter-vs-facebook-vs-google-buzz-36709 date accessed 10/10/2015

86 Sinnett, A. P., *Esoteric Buddhism (5th ed.)*, Houghton Mifflin., (1884). p 127

87 http://www.cjmartes.com/cjmartes_akashicfield.asp date accessed 01/12/2015

88 http://www.soulsofdistortion.nl/SODA_chapter4.html date accessed 01/12/2015

89 Edgar Cayce Reading 1650-1

90 http://www.realsuperpowers.com/edgar-cayce

91 http://www.near-death.com/experiences/cayce01.html

92 Wilmshurst, W. L., *The Meaning of Masonry*, Lund, Humphries & Co., LTD, Bradford and London, 1922, p. 97

From darkness – light – *pages 126-137*

93 https://archive.org/stream/GeraldMassey-Lectures/GeraldMassey-lectures_djvu.txt date accessed 22/03/2016

94 http://www.heartnsoul.com/cayce_NDEs.htm date accessed 22/03/2016

95 http://www.nderf.org/NDERF/NDE_Experiences/michael_f_nde.htm date accessed 01/10/2015

To see or not see – the All-Seeing Eye – *pages 138-143*

96 http://www.gotquestions.org/all-seeing-eye.html#ixzz3SmXubIBS date accessed 20/09/2015

97 http://en.wikipedia.org/wiki/Aachen_Cathedral date accessed 20/09/2015

98 Gensler, H. J., *Formal Ethics*. Routledge, New York, 1996

99 http://www.richardcassaro.com/occult-symbolism-behind-pine-cone-art-architecture date accessed 25/04/2015

100 http://plato.stanford.edu/entries/pineal-gland/ date accessed 25/04/2015

101 http://www.chakrahub.com/6th-chakra date accessed 25/04/2015

No bones about it – the Skull and Crossbones – *pages 144-152*

102 A tracing board is a picture containing the various emblems and symbols of Freemasonry. Tracing board lectures are delivered to the Candidate following each of the three degrees. Operatively a tracing board was used by builders to draw their designs upon.

103 http://www.healthline.com/human-body-maps/femur date accessed 16/12/2015

104 www.numerologystars.com/number-6-meaning/ date accessed 16/12/2015

105 www.bje.org.au/learning/hebrew/alphabet/06vav.html date accessed 16/12/2015

106 http://www.joyousworld.com/qabalah/words/letternames/05vav.html 04/12/2015

107 Barrett, F., *The Magus*, London, 1801, p 132

Love rocks – the Ashlars – *pages 00-00*

108 http://en.wikipedia.org/wiki/Kaaba date accessed 29/03/2015

109 http://www.examiner.com/article/cube-symbolism-and-the-ancient-wisdom date accessed 28/03/2015

110 http://www.theguardian.com/commentisfree/2012/dec/13/what-is-love-five-theories date accessed 18/02/2015

Index

A

Abbot, Bud   164
Acupuncture   75
Aetius   150
Akashic Records, The   120-124, 139
Alcmaeon, of Croton   17, 87
Aldrin, Buzz   164
All-Seeing Eye, The   54, 138-143
Amygdala   76-78
Apron, Masonic lambskin   40-48, 59, 145, 157
Apuleius   111
Aristotle   10, 12, 14, 22, 68, 92
Ark of the Covenant   91
Awareness   159

B

Bacon, Roger   13
Bailey, Alice Ann   121
Balance, Achieving; Necessity of   32, 50-52, 55, 68, 71, 79, 84, 100, 102-103, 105-106, 111, 131-132, 135, 141-143
Beehive   14, 22, 24, 25, 82-89, 157
Bhagavad Gita   11, 61
Bindi   142
Blanc, Mel   164
Blavatsky, Helena Petrovna   43, 120,
Blazing Star   28, 100, 105
Borgnine, Ernest   164
Bradman, Sir Donald   166
Brain, human   17, 23, 26, 30, 45, 48, 52-54, 66-67, 71, 76, 98, 110, 114, 129, 141, 145-148, 151-152, 155
Brett, Francis   150
Bruner, Jerome   92
Buddha, Gautama Siddhartha   15, 16, 40, 68, 81, 84, 135, 158

C

Cable Tow   33-39, 147
Calcott, Wellins   111
Cave of the Bee   83
Cayce, Edgar   103, 122-123, 130
Chakra, Sixth   142
Chapin, Edwin Hubbell   120
Churchill, Winston   22, 95, 164
Circadian rhythm   53-54
Circumambulation, Rite of   126
Confucius   13, 15, 26, 94, 118, 135, 139, 160
Craft, The   13
Creation; of the world; Adam and Eve   101
Cube   25, 153-158

D

Death   80, 87, 127, 129, 130, 144-152
de Mello, Anthony   96
DeMille, Cecille B.   164
Descartes, Rene   142, 146
Divine Spark   12, 27-32, 39, 43, 45, 47, 48, 67, 69, 70, 71, 76, 77, 110, 115, 135, 146, 149, 152, 156, 157, 158, 163
Doyle, Sir Arthur Conan   165
Duality   51, 68, 101, 105, 126, 127, 129, 132, 133
Duodenum   31

E

Eddy, Mary Baker   66
Eden, Garden of   41
Edward VII, King   166
Edward VIII, King   166
Ego   12, 21, 30, 35, 38, 39, 77, 142, 146, 157
Einstein, Albert   87, 119, 147
Elway, John   166
Energy   26, 27, 28, 32, 42, 45, 47, 53, 66-67,

69, 71, 75, 76, 81, 104, 106, 107, 110, 112, 119, 120, 122, 123, 128, 130, 132, 147, 150, 156
Enoch; Vaults of   29-30
Entered Apprentice   43, 47, 57, 59, 65, 74, 92, 153
Epictetus   17, 80
Essenes, The   22, 41, 112
Eye of Horus, The   138
Eye of Wisdom, The   140-141
Ex Tenebris Lux   12

F
F.E.A.R.   135
Faith   30, 34-39, 79, 96-98, 114, 115, 131, 157
Femur Bone   148
Fibonacci sequence   92-93, 142
Flesh   8, 26, 44, 60, 66, 70, 146, 158
Ford, President Gerald   164
Franklin, Benjamin   164-165
Fujiyoshi, Hiroto   84

G
Gable, Clark   165
Gavel, Common   24, 57-63, 113, 153, 157, 167
Geometry   27, 29, 51, 92-93, 156
George IV, King   166
George VI, King   166
Golden Mean Spiral; Golden Mean Geometry   92-93
Golden Rule, The   15, 46, 68, 69, 94-95, 139, 160, 161

H
Hall, Manly P.   31, 150
Happy Gilmore   115
Hardy, Oliver   165
Hartmann, Franz MD   45-46
Harpocrates   111
Heaven   37, 45, 51, 101, 110, 111, 121, 130, 131, 149, 156
Heaven; what is   110, 130

Hermetic Principles, The Seven   103-104
Hermes Trismegistus   103
Hesychia   112
Hilel   16, 94, 139
Houdini, Harry   165
Huxley, Aldous   12
Hypothalamus   53, 76

I
Illuminati   24, 25
Illumination   12, 14, 44, 76-77, 86, 98, 134, 143, 145, 154, 157
Initiate; Initiation   33, 34, 41, 105, 111, 112
INRI   157
Internalisation, Meaning of   162

J
Jacob, Biblical character   70, 149
Jesus, of Nazareth; Christ   12, 16, 42, 84, 94, 110-112, 133, 157, 158, 160
Jimmo, Ryan   166
Job, Biblical Character   159-160
John, the Baptist   67
John Chrysostom   84
John, the Evangelist   67
Jung, Carl   12, 26

K
Kaaba   156
Karate   12, 96, 99, 134
Kennedy, Graham   166
King Jr, Martin Luther   96
Kipling, Rudyard   55, 165
Knowledge   11, 12-13, 14, 22, 26, 33, 43, 45, 47, 48, 52, 61, 64, 83, 86, 88, 89, 91, 93, 96, 97, 98, 110, 111, 113, 116, 120, 121, 122, 123, 124, 126, 128, 129, 130, 132-137, 142, 143, 144, 145, 147, 148, 149, 158, 159
Know Thyself, adage   9-11
Kybalion, The   104

L
Lao Tzu   11, 13-14, 16, 22, 102, 159

Law of Conservation of Energy, The   119
Law of Motion, Newton's   12, 102,
Lawry, Bill   166
Leadbeater, C.W.   121
Lesser Lights of Freemasonry   131
Lewis, C.S.   12, 54
Life, Meaning of   9
Light; Masonic Light   12, 16, 33, 34, 86, 88, 102, 126-137
Lindbergh, Charles   165
Lloyd, Sir Clive   165
Love   21, 24, 27, 34, 35, 38, 44, 46, 104, 106, 130, 131, 155, 157-158, 160-161
Luke, Gospel of   43, 61

M

Mackey, Albert   65, 96, 131
Madu Purnima   84
Mahavira   17, 60
Mark Master, degree   85
Massey, Gerald   128
Matthew, Gospel of   43, 94, 110, 111, 112, 133, 161
Mayne, Thomas   166
McArthur, Douglas   165
Meditation   15, 17, 31, 112, 114, 115, 128, 155, 161
Memento Mori   151
Mevlevi School of Dervishes   112
Mezger, Guy   166
Michelangelo   62, 156
Miletich, Pat   8, 166
Mosaic Pavement; Checkerboard   51, 100-107, 126, 157

N

Near Death Experience (NDE)   129-131
Newton, Isaac   12, 41, 68, 102

O

Omphalos, stone   83, 84, 86, 87
O'Neal, Shaquille   166

P

Paisley, Brad   166
Palmer, Arnold   165
Pencil   8, 22, 25, 82, 118-125, 167
Pike, Albert   31, 51, 86, 90
Pineal Gland   54, 66, 141-142, 146, 149, 151
Pippen, Scottie   166
Plato   10, 12, 14, 16, 22, 82, 94, 112, 138, 156
Platonic Solids   156
Point Within a Circle   26, 64-72, 157, 158
Ponsford, Bill   166
Porphyry, of Tyre   83
Postcard Masons   20, 74
Prayer, what is   112
Principle of Polarity, The   104
Pryor, Richard   166
Psalms, Book of   115, 121
Pyramid, Giza   58
Pythagoras   13, 16, 22, 24, 111, 118, 128, 160
Pythagorean System; School; Community   28, 41, 87, 112, 150
Pythia   10, 83

R

Reading, importance of   160
R.E.A.L.   135
Revelations, Book of   45, 121
Richards, Michael   166
Robinson, Sugar Ray   165
Rogers, Roy   165
Roosevelt, President Theodore   165
Royal Arch; Royal Arch of Solomon; Holy Royal Arch   29, 85

S

Saint John Chrysostom   84
Saint Symeon, The New Theologian   112
Sanctum Sanctorum   91, 146
Secret Society 19-26, 108
Sellers, Peter   37, 166
Seven Sages, The   9 - 10
Seven Wise Men; Seven Sages   9
Shintoism   95

Sickels, Daniel   113
Simpson, Bobby   166
Sinnett, Alfred Percy   121
Six, the number   149-150
Skirrett   82, 118, 153, 154, 167
Skull   145-148
Socrates   10-12, 118, 134
Solar Plexus   30
Sol Invictus   127
Sophocles   83
Soul   12, 13, 24, 26, 44, 48, 49, 58, 61, 66-69, 74, 83, 85-87, 88, 89, 91, 98, 103, 105, 110, 113, 122, 130, 131, 133, 135, 142, 146-152, 154, 156, 158, 159, 163
Sphere   148
Square and Compasses   18, 24, 27, 28, 31, 51, 70, 108, 132, 151
Staircase, Winding   29, 90-99, 113, 142, 162
Steinmatz, George H.   85
Sun, The   25, 51, 65, 67, 127-128, 131-133, 136, 137
Sunlight, Benefits of; Danger of   127
Supreme Being   12, 28, 123
Sutcliffe, Herbert   165
Suture, brain   144
Symeon, Saint; The New Theologian   18, 112

T
Temple, of Apollo   9 - 10, 82, 85
Temple, King Solomon's   28, 90-92, 100
Tepoxtecatl   41
Thales of Miletus   10-11
Theoria   112
Theosophy   34, 43
Therapeutic communities   112
Third Eye   141
Thoth   103
Three Great Lights in Freemasonry   132
Tracing (Trestle) Board   64, 109, 144
Transcendence   33, 46, 159
Triangle; Equilateral; Right-angle   16, 24, 25, 28, 40, 43, 45, 47, 50-52, 84, 132, 138, 149
Trowel   24, 25, 82, 153, 154, 167

Twain, Mark   165
Twenty-four (24) inch gauge   24, 49-56, 57, 59, 153, 157
Tyler   42, 73-81, 165

U
Universal Law; Nature's Law   46, 52, 68-69, 71, 85, 88, 93, 95, 96, 139-140, 142, 160

V
Vatican, The   141
VAV, Hebrew letter   150
Vices   57, 58-59, 62
Visible Light Spectrum   42
Virtues of Freemasonry, Three   131
Vitruvian Man, Da Vinci's   150-151
Vitruvius, Marcus   150-151

W
Walker, Fred   166
Warner, Harry   165
Wayne, John   165
Wicca   95
Wilde, Oscar   165
William IV, King   166
Wilmshurst, W.L.   12, 123
Wisdom   134-135, 136
Worldly Eye   140-141

X
X, Meaning of; Roman numeral   148-151
Xun Zi   18, 60

Y
Yin and Yang   52, 70, 101-103, 106

Z
Zain, C.C.   87
Zeitgebers   53-54
Zoroastrianism   95

BV - #0023 - 210223 - C0 - 229/152/10 - PB - 9780853185239 - Gloss Lamination